READING
FOR WORKPLACE SUCCESS

GENERAL BUSINESS

ROSEMARIE J. PARK, Ed.D.
University of Minnesota
Minneapolis, MN

REBECCA L. OLSON
East End Adult Education Center
Cincinnati, OH

NEILD B. OLDHAM
Writer, Consultant
New London, CT

Consulting Editor:
David J. Pucel, Ph.D.
University of Minnesota

PARADIGM

ABOUT THE AUTHORS

Rosemarie J. Park is an associate professor of education at the University of Minnesota. She holds an Ed.D. in reading from the Harvard Graduate School of Education and has taught adult literacy in Great Britain and the United States. She has researched, written, and presented extensively in the areas of adult literacy and reading in the workplace with a focus on the educational needs of the workplace and the assessment of basic skills as they relate to hiring and promotion. In addition, she has served as a training consultant in private industry and contributed to numerous national and international forums and symposia, including those sponsored by the U.S. Department of Education, the International Reading Association, and the MacArthur Foundation.

Rebecca L. Olson is executive director of the East End Adult Education Center in Cincinnati, Ohio, which offers adult literacy instruction and GED preparation. She has an M.S. in Reading Education from Purdue University with a focus on adult and secondary reading education and is a Ph.D. candidate in adult education at the University of Minnesota. She has years of experience teaching disadvantaged adults. In addition, she has evaluated and consulted for adult and occupational literacy programs and is widely published in the areas of adult education and occupational literacy.

Neild B. Oldham is a writer and consultant specializing in education. He has taught writing, book publishing, and computer courses at the post-secondary level and has authored several books. He was director of editorial services for the School Division of the McGraw-Hill Book Company and currently owns and operates The Oldham Publishing Service.

David J. Pucel, Consulting Editor, is professor and head of the division of industrial education, Department of Vocational and Technical Education, University of Minnesota. His degrees are in industrial education from the University of Wisconsin-Stout (B.A.), vocational education from the University of Illinois (M.A.), and education from the University of Minnesota (Ph.D.). He has conducted research, presented, and published extensively on instructional design, teaching and evaluation in vocational education, and training in business and industry, and he is an authority on performance-based instruction.

Editor: **Art Lyons**
Production: **The Oldham Publishing Service**
Illustrator: **Tom Lochray**

Acknowledgements: Material on page 349 adapted from *Small Business Management and Entrepreneurship* by Olive D. Church, SRA, 1984. pp 290-2. Material on page 350-1 adapted from *Working at Human Relations*, 2e, by Rosemary T. Fruehling and Neild B. Oldham, Paradigm Publishing International, 1991. pp. 176-8. Material on page 176 adapted from *Basic Telemarketing: Skills for Sales and Service Productivity*, Mary D. Pekas, Paradigm Publishing International, p. 110.

Library of Congress Cataloging-in-Publication Data
Park, Rosemarie J.
  Reading for workplace success: general business / by Rosemarie J. Park, Rebecca L. Olson and Neild B. Oldham.
    p.351 cm.
  ISBN 1-56118-200-1
  1. Readers—Business. 2. English language—Business English. 3. Business enterprises—Problems, exercises, etc. I. Olson, Rebecca L. II. Title.
  PE1127.B86P37   1991
  428.6'02465—dc20

Printed in the United States

10 9 8 7 6 5 4 3 2 1

TABLE OF CONTENTS

TO THE STUDENT

Reading may not be your major responsibility on the job. However, you cannot work through an average week, or often an average day, without having to read something.

Your job performance will depend, at least in part, on your ability to understand written communications.

Some of the reading tasks you must do on the job are

- ✔ read letters, memos, notes from coworkers, supervisors, or customers
- ✔ read company policy manuals
- ✔ read operation manuals to understand how to run office equipment
- ✔ read requests for information, goods, and services
- ✔ read reports on company activities or the activities of your coworkers

You must be able to read such things as the directions on a job application form so you can fill it out properly. Also, you must read to understand the details of your health insurance and other benefits.

What Will This Book Teach You?

This book will teach you to read better in a work setting. This book uses the kinds of reading you will find in a general business settings. The reading strategies you use when you read this book are the strategies you will find in vocational training or on a job.

As you work through this book, you will

- ✔ use a problem-solving strategy to improve your reading
- ✔ read a variety of business documents, forms, and graphics
- ✔ apply selected business concepts to your reading
- ✔ read information accurately and completely
- ✔ identify what is important and what is not important to read for the task
- ✔ take correct action based on what you read
- ✔ read and respond to information from supervisors, coworkers, and customers
- ✔ practice basic word skills

What Does It Mean To Be A Good Reader?

To be a good reader, you must read accurately, completely, and clearly. This means you must be able to relate what you read to the task at hand. After reading, you must be able to take the correct action. Good readers view reading as problem solving. You will become a good reader and problem solver by using the problem-solving strategy presented in this book. The next section, "How Good Problem Solvers Think About Reading," describes this strategy in detail.

How Will This Book Help You Learn To Read?

This book will present you with a variety of situations and business problems. Your job will be to use reading to solve those problems the best way you can. You will learn to study a problem and plan the best way to solve it before you start reading. Then your reading and problem-solving abilities will improve as you practice in many different situations.

Each lesson will

✔ show you how other people have solved problems through their own reading

✔ introduce you to new information, which you can combine with what you already know to help you make decisions about your reading

✔ guide you through the problem-solving strategy before asking you to do it on your own

✔ help review basic word skills and provide you the opportunity to check your progress along the way

✔ ask you a series of questions that will help you solve problems

Now study the next section, "How Good Problem Solvers Think About Reading." This section will discuss in more detail the problem-solving strategy you will practice throughout this book. It will also introduce you to some of the decisions you have to make as you read, and it will help you make those decisions.

After studying the next section carefully, refer back to it whenever you need to as you work through the book.

HOW GOOD
PROBLEM SOLVERS
THINK ABOUT READING

You have only one reason for reading on the job: to solve problems. Whether you are reading memos from supervisors, reading company policy manuals, or reading operation manuals to understand how to run a machine, the reading you do will solve—or help solve—a business problem, big or small.

In this section, you will learn the problem-solving strategy you will use throughout this book. As you work through the book, you will apply this strategy to a variety of problems.

Here is a small problem whose solution requires reading:

Work Problem

Your supervisor calls a meeting of all workers in the office. He hands out an article called "Organize for Productivity." He says, "We've been looking for ways to improve productivity. This article has some simple but good ideas. I'd like everyone to read this and try to carry out the suggestions." You read the document.

Organize for Productivity

An effective way to increase your productivity is by being neat and organized. Here are a few simple steps you can take to achieve this:

Avoid having piles of papers on your desk in which messages and important information can get buried.

Use clearly labeled files, which can be kept in vertical holders on your desk if needed constantly.

Record appointments, deadlines, assignments on a wall or desk calendar.

Keep a "to do" list.

Make notes on full-sized paper. Never use scraps of paper, which can easily be lost.

Write notes right on copies of letters and memos so all information is in one spot.

Keep only what you need on your desk to do your work promptly and professionally.

To work through problems such as this and those you will find throughout this book, do what good problem solvers do: follow the problem-solving strategy described below.

Overview

Step 1:

Define Your Problem

Good problem solvers find the best solution possible to the problem. Before reading, they ask themselves these two questions:

> *What is my purpose for reading this material?*
>
> *What should I be able to do when I finish?*

Step 2:

Plan Your Solution

In this part of the strategy, problem solvers ask questions that help them determine what to read and how to read it:

> *What information do I need from this material to solve my work problem?*
>
> *How carefully will I have to read to find the information I need?*

Step 3:

Read

Problem solvers combine their planning with their reading skills—their knowledge of sentences and word meanings. How they read, what they read, indeed, whether they read at all depends on how they answered the questions in Steps 1 and 2 above. Regardless of their purpose for reading, problem solvers always try to answer these four questions:

> *What information do the format clues give me?*
>
> *What do I already know about this situation that will help me?*
>
> *Should I continue reading this material?*
>
> *What information is important because it helps me solve my work problem?*

If the purpose for reading is more than simply finding information, problem solvers ask other questions as well when they read. When the purpose for reading is to find how to carry out a task, problem solvers ask

> *Have I organized the information to help me carry out the directions?*

When the purpose for reading is to check or confirm information, problem solvers ask

> *Have I compared the new information with the original information.*

When the purpose for reading is to draw a conclusion or make a decision, problem solvers ask

> *Have I put the new and old information together to draw a conclusion?*

Step 4:

Check Your Solution

Problem solvers are not finished just because they are finished reading. They must review the problem and make sure that their reading has provided a good solution. At this point, problem solvers always ask themselves the following questions:

Did I accomplish my purpose?

Did the information help me solve my work problem? How?

If they answer "yes" to these two questions, they are finished. If they answer "no," they must review the problem and the strategy they worked through to see where they made a mistake.

Making Decisions about Your Reading

Each of the questions in the problem-solving strategy above requires you to make a decision about your reading. Let's look at the decisions you have to make and discuss how you should make them. As you work through the book, do not hesitate to look back to this section for help as often as you need to.

Each time you work through the problem-solving strategy, you begin with a work problem. If there is no problem, then there is no reason to read. Here is the work problem you read earlier.

Work Problem

Your supervisor calls a meeting of all workers in the office. He hands out an article called "Organize for Productivity." He says, "We've been looking for ways to improve productivity. This article has some simple but good ideas. I'd like everyone to read this and try to carry out the suggestions." You read the document.

Organize for Productivity

An effective way to increase your productivity is by being neat and organized. Here are a few simple steps you can take to achieve this:

Avoid having piles of papers on your desk in which messages and important information can get buried.

Use clearly labeled files, which can be kept in vertical holders on your desk if needed constantly.

Record appointments, deadlines, assignments on a wall or desk calendar.

Keep a "to do" list.

Make notes on full-sized paper. Never use scraps of paper, which can easily be lost.

Write notes right on copies of letters and memos so all information is in one spot.

Keep only what you need on your desk to do your work promptly and professionally.

Define Your Problem

What is my purpose for reading this material?

There are not as many *general* purposes for reading as you might think. Most workers read for one of four reasons:

1. To find information
2. To find directions or explanations for how to do something
3. To check or confirm information
4. To draw a conclusion or make a decision

For the work problem above, your purpose is *to find directions or explanations for how to do something.*

What should I be able to do when I finish?

This question simply asks you to think ahead to why you are reading. It will help you check your solution later.

In this case, you are reading *to find out how to be more productive.*

Plan Your Solution

What information do I need from this material to solve my work problem?

This question asks you to think about what you must get out of your reading to solve the work problem. Your answer to this question will help you answer the following question in this planning step.

In this case, *you need information about keeping your desk organized and neat.*

How carefully will I have to read to find the information I need?

This question suggests that you will not always need to read everything carefully. How carefully you must read depends on your purpose.

In the work problem above, *you should read carefully to find what your supervisor thinks will help make you a more productive worker.*

Read

What information do the format clues give me?

In this work problem, the heading tells you that you can organize yourself to be a better worker.

What do I already know about this situation that will help me?

The supervisor is interested in improving productivity. You also know how much your current work habits match your boss's suggestions.

Should I continue reading this material?	Yes, to be sure you can follow the directions.
What information is important because it helps me solve my work problem?	All of the specific things you can do to organize your desk and work.
Have I organized the information to help me carry out the directions?	You can number and list the steps for organizing your desk to be sure you know them.

Check Your Solution

Did I accomplish my purpose? (Did I organize the information to carry out the directions?)	Once you have read something you believe solves the work problem, think about why you read (your purpose) to make sure you have accomplished your purpose.
Did the information help me solve my work problem? How?	A final check. To answer this question, you must review the problem. You may find at times that your reading does not solve the problem.
	In this case, you are able to carry out the steps in the article; your reading has solved the work problem.

Let's look at the problem-solving strategy once more:

Step 1: Define Your Problem

> What is my purpose for reading this material?

> What should I be able to do when I finish?

Step 2: Plan Your Solution

> What information do I need from this material to solve my work problem?

> How carefully will I have to read to find the information I need?

Step 3: Read

> What information do the format clues give me?

> What do I already know about this situation that will help me?

> Should I continue reading this material?

> What information is important because it helps me solve my work problem?

Step 4: Check Your Solution

> Did I accomplish my purpose?

> Did the information help me solve my work problem? How?

UNIT I

READING TO FIND
INFORMATION

At work, you will often need to read to find information. When is the meeting? Where is it? What must be sent? How long will it take? To find information, you will read all sorts of material—memos, manuals, shipping forms, and maps are just a few.

In Unit I, you will learn the reading steps used to find important information in what you read and to ignore unnecessary information. These reading steps include the following:

1. Look for information that the format provides.

2. Think about what you already know about this situation that will help you.

3. Decide whether to continue reading the material.

4. Pick out the information that helps you solve your work problem.

Comfort Line Furniture Company

In Unit I, you will work first at Comfort Line Furniture Company, which sells quality furniture to department stores. You will work with Penny Smith, the sales manager, and several other employees in the sales department. You will also work with Randy Fuller, the office manager.

Next you will work at Leisure Stores, a chain of stores selling toys, games, electronics, and sports equipment. You will meet Leslie Snow and Fred Conti, two buyers, and Al Gomez, manager of the toy department.

Your next company will be Ace Public Accounting Company. You will work with Jane Florio, an accountant.

Your last company will be Mailmart, a large company that sells sporting goods and clothing. At the end of each unit you will return to Mailmart. In this unit, you will work with Darcy Turner, sales manager.

Memos are a common form of reading material in a business. *Memo* is short for *memorandum.* Companies use memos to pass on specific, up-to-date information about meetings, tasks, decisions, or schedules. Memos often replace spoken communication because they provide a written record of the information.

Most memos have a similar format or organization. This makes them easy to read. The memo format highlights important facts. Here is a typical memo.

DATE:	January 11, 199—
TO:	Penny Smith, Marketing Director
FROM:	Rob Barnes, Sales Manager
SUBJECT:	MEETING WITH SALES REPS

I have scheduled our meeting with the sales representatives for tomorrow. The meeting will be in conference room 4 on the second floor. It will start at 2:00 p.m.

Here is the agenda. I would like to discuss the following items:

 1. travel budgets
 2. the new catalog
 3. the report form

al
attachment
c: M. Morri

Labels:

Date it was written

Who it is to

Who sent it

What it is about

The text: writer's message

Initials of typist

If copies being sent to others

if additional material is being sent with memo

3

Reading to Find Information

Now look at the memo again and see how Penny Smith reads it.

1. She looks for information from the format clues. (It is dated today. It is from Rob Barnes, the sales manager. It is about a meeting.)

2. She looks for what she already knows about this situation that will help her. (She may be familiar with problems in the sales department that could be discussed at the meeting.)

3. She decides whether to continue reading this material. (Yes, she finds out that a meeting is scheduled for tomorrow at 2 p.m. with the sales reps.)

4. She identifies the information that helps her solve her work problem. (The date, time, place, and agenda of the meeting.)

```
DATE:       January 11, 199-
TO:         Penny Smith,
            Marketing Director
FROM:       Rob Barnes, Sales Manager
SUBJECT:  MEETING WITH SALES REPS

I have scheduled our meeting with
the sales representatives for
tomorrow.  The meeting will be in
conference room 4 on the second
floor.  It will start at 2:00 p.m.

Here is the agenda.  I would like
to discuss the following items:


  1. travel budgets
  2. the new catalog
  3. the report form



al
attachment
c: M. Morri
```

Penny Smith read to find information in a memo. Before reading, she used the problem-solving strategy for reading introduced on pages viii to xii.

Let's go through another work problem using the problem-solving strategy.

Work Problem

You are starting a new job as assistant to Penny Smith, marketing director for Comfort Line Furniture Co. Ms. Smith asks you to sort through some memos and find the one that is about the new line of chairs. When you find it, you must give it to her.

You know the memo gives information on styles and materials and is from Donald Regis in the materials department. You pick up the memo below and read it. Does it have the information Ms. Smith is looking for?

DATE: January 12, 199—

TO: Penny Smith, Marketing Director

FROM: Donald Regis, Materials Department

SUBJECT: CHAIRS

Here is some information on our new line of chairs.

The dining room chairs have straight backs. We also are working on a new easy chair.

There are two choices of materials for the dining room chair seat. One will be a plastic material that is good for families with small children. The other material is a heavy cotton for more formal use. The easy chair will be covered in leather.

The new desk chair with the adjustable back should be comfortable for both tall and short people. It will be ready next month. It has a cloth seat.

The old line of easy chairs did not have a model covered with leather. We just had several choices of cloth.

Define Your Problem

What is my purpose for reading this material?

To find out if it has the information Ms. Smith needs.

What should I be able to do when I finish reading?

If it has the information, give it to Ms. Smith.

Plan Your Solution

What information do I need from this material to solve my work problem?

Styles and materials in the new line of chairs.

How carefully will I have to read to find the information I need?

Carefully, to find out if it has what Ms. Smith wants to see.

Read

What information do the format clues give me?

Who it is sent to, who sent it, on what date it was sent, and what it is about.

What do I already know about this situation that will help me?

The memo will be from Donald Regis. It will have information on the new line of chairs.

Should I continue reading this material?

Yes, for information on styles and materials.

What information is important because it helps me solve my work problem?

It has information on styles and materials for new dining room chair, easy chair, and desk chair.

Check Your Solution

Did I accomplish my purpose? (What information did I find?)

Yes. I found that this memo has the information Ms. Smith needs.

Did the information help me solve my work problem? How?

Yes. I can give this memo to Ms. Smith.

Problem-Solving Practice

Now apply your reading strategy to another work problem.

Work Problem

Ms. Smith will be away most of today. She says "I am expecting an important memo from Alex Burn, the West Coast regional sales manager. It will be about his sales trip to Los Angeles for the annual furniture convention. Please read everything that comes in. If Mr Burn's memo comes, put it on my desk. I will read it when I get back this afternoon."

DATE: March 9, 199—

TO: Penny Smith, Marketing Director

FROM: Alex Burn, West Coast Sales Manager

SUBJECT: ANNUAL FURNITURE CONVENTION

This convention was held in Los Angeles on February 24-28.

At least 25,000 people attended. Buyers from every major hotel and motel chain were there. Some department store buyers were there also. It looked to me as if companies were taking in some big orders.

I met with several buyers to show them our new line of tables. The response was very favorable. Several people want a sales rep to call with more information. My feeling is that we have a winner here. Let's hope I am right. We will have a better idea of how it will sell in a few months.

I think we should have an exhibit here next year. We must reserve a booth by May 4. Can we decide soon? The person in charge of booths is Bernie Bly 213-555-9911. Call if you have questions.

Define Your Problem

What is my purpose for reading this material?

_____

_____

What should I be able to do when I finish reading?

_____

_____

Plan Your Solution

What information do I need from this
material to solve my work problem?

_____

_____

_____

_____

How carefully will I have to read to find
the information I need?

_____

_____

_____

Read

What information do the format clues
give me?

_____

_____

_____

_____

What do I already know about this
situation that will help me?

_____

_____

_____

_____

Should I continue reading this material?

_____

_____

What information is important because
it helps me solve my work problem?

_____

_____

_____

Check Your Solution

Did I accomplish my purpose? (What
information did I find?)

_____

_____

_____

_____

Did the information help me solve my
work problem? How?

_____

_____

_____

_____

Answers to the Problem-Solving Practice questions are on pages 20-21.

On Your Own

Here are four more work problems. Remember to define your purpose and plan your solution. Read memos carefully and check to see if you have solved your problem.

Work Problem A

Ms. Smith tells you, "I must decide about exhibiting at the furniture convention next year. I've asked the sales representatives to let me know what they think. Read the comments from Terry Marks and let me know if she thinks we should exhibit. I'd also like to know her reasons."

```
DATE:      April 3, 199—

TO:        Penny Smith, Marketing Director

FROM:      Terry Marks, Sales Representative

RE:        EXHIBITING AT CONVENTION
```

Alex Burn told me why he thinks we should exhibit at the furniture convention next year. I disagree with him.

Hotels and motels buy large quantities of beds and chairs that are sturdy but not too expensive. Comfort Line has always produced smaller amounts of higher quality goods.

We have a large design department that keeps up with market trends. This means we do well selling to interior decorators and better department stores. Our current market may suffer if we change our focus to motel chains.

Right now we are not prepared to make furniture for the hotel/motel market. I don't think it makes sense to spend money to exhibit at the convention.

What is your purpose for reading this memo?

_____

_____

Does Terry Marks want the company to have an exhibit? Why?

_____

_____

What sort of customers does Comfort Line sell to most often? Why?

_____

_____

Work Problem B

Carla Hernandez is the vice president for sales and marketing. She will make the final decision about exhibiting at the furniture convention next year. The choices are to have no exhibit, to have a small display, or to have a full size one. She will base her decision on the information from the sales reps and Alex Burn.

A memo arrives for Ms. Smith from Ms. Hernandez. Ms. Smith asks you to read it and tell her what decision Ms. Hernandez made.

```
DATE:     April 25, 199—

TO:       Penny Smith, Marketing Director

FROM:     Carla Hernandez, Vice President,
          Sales and Marketing

SUBJECT: EXHIBITING AT CONVENTION

I am glad your sales team is eager to push
Comfort Line into new markets.  However,
Ms. Marks is right about the hotel/motel
market.  We are not now producing for it.
I do not want to spend the money for a
full-size booth.  They are very expensive.

I think we can spend a little money to
find out more about it.  Let's reserve a
small display booth next year.  It will
give us a chance to gather information.
We can see who else is selling there, meet
the key people who buy, and begin to get a
feel for the market.

Please contact Mr. Bly, the convention
organizer, to reserve a small booth.

Alex Burn should plan to be there when the
hotel purchasing agents meet.
```

What is your purpose for reading this memo?

_____

_____

Does Ms. Hernandez want to display at the convention? Why?

_____

_____

Who does she want to be at the convention to meet with the purchasing agents?

_____

_____

Work Problem C

After getting Carla Hernandez's decision, Ms. Smith shows you a memo. She says, "Here's the memo I'm sending to all the sales reps to tell them the final decision on the convention." She asks you to read it, too, so you'll know what to tell anybody who calls with questions.

```
DATE:     April 21, 199—
TO:       All Sales Representatives
FROM:     Penny Smith, Marketing Director
SUBJECT:  FURNITURE CONVENTION EXHIBIT

We will exhibit at the annual furniture
convention next year with a small display
booth.

As you know, we have different opinions in
the department about whether we should
move into this market.  It is important
for you all to understand how this
decision was made and to know our goal for
exhibiting.

I am including several memos for you to
read.  Two are from sales representatives
who have opposite views on the subject.
The other explains the final decision.
Please call my assistant if you have
questions or want to schedule time to talk
with me about this.


attachments
```

What is your purpose for reading this memo?

_____

_____

What attachments are being sent with this memo?

_____

_____

Why is Ms. Smith sending the attachments?

_____

_____

Work Problem D

Ms. Smith is promoted to vice president for sales and marketing. She asks you to continue as her assistant. This is a good opportunity for you to increase your responsibilities. You have just moved into your new office and are sorting her mail. She is interviewing people to succeed her as marketing director. Here is one of the memos you read.

```
DATE:      October 22, 199—

TO:        Penny Smith, Vice President
           Sales and Marketing

FROM:      Albert Cortez, President

SUBJECT:   CONGRATULATIONS

Congratulations on your promotion! I know
we made a good choice!

I want to introduce you to the board of
directors at their upcoming meeting, which
is 4 p.m. next Friday (Oct. 29).  It is
important that they meet you personally.

I would also like you to have breakfast or
lunch that day with Marty Burroughs, the
board chairperson.  Please ask your
assistant to call my office to confirm
that you got these messages.


c: Martin Burroughs
```

What is your purpose for reading this memo?

_____

_____

What are the president's reasons for sending the memo?

_____

_____

Does the memo contain information Ms. Smith needs to see today? Why?

_____

_____

What must you tell your boss about the president's message?

_____

_____

Skills Practice: Finding a Word's Meaning

As you read to solve work problems, you will often see words you do not understand. This is normal. Even the most experienced readers see words they do not understand. When this happens, do not just skip the word. Its meaning might be important to solving your work problem.

There are three ways readers learn the meaning of a new word.

1. Check the sentence and paragraph in which the word is found for clues to its meaning.
2. Check the parts of the word for clues to its meaning.
3. Check with an expert or a dictionary.

In this lesson, you will learn about the first way to find a word's meaning: checking the context.

You can often find an unfamiliar word's meaning from the sentence and paragraph in which you find it. The words in the sentence or paragraph will help you decide the meaning of the new word. Even the type of document you are reading can give you clues. Also, check against what you already know about a subject.

Example: In the memo from Donald Regis to Perry Smith, you read,

> The new desk chair with the *adjustable* back should be comfortable for both tall and short people.

The word *adjustable* tells you something about the back of the chair. What might make it comfortable for tall and short people? Being able to move the back up or down might help. *Adjustable* means "to change to make fit." This chair has a back that can be changed to make it fit different people.

Example: In the memo from Mr. Barnes, you read this sentence:

> Here is the *agenda*. I would like to discuss the following items

You may have never seen the word *agenda* before. If not, you can decide from its context what it means. The memo is about a meeting. The next sentence introduces the items to discuss. This tells you that *agenda* means a list of things to talk about at a meeting.

Example: In the memo from Mr. Cortez, you read this sentence:

> Please ask your assistant to call my office to *confirm* that you got these messages.

Even if you did not know the word *confirm*, the rest of the sentence suggests that it means to firm up or make sure. In this case the president wants to be sure that Ms. Smith has received the memo and knows about the meeting and the breakfast.

Exercise A

Read the following sentences. On the blank lines to the right, write what the word in italics means based on the sentence.

1. We *concentrate* on department stores as the best market for our furniture.

   _____

2. If you receive any complaints, please *refer* them to the customer service department.

   _____

3. I think we have *implemented* everything you asked us to.

   _____

4. The numbers in the memo *correspond* with the numbers you will find on the order form.

   _____

5. My *initial* thought is that is a good idea. I may change my mind later.

   _____

Answers to Skills Practice Exercise A are on page 21.

Exercise B

Read the following sentences. On the blank lines to the right of each, write what the word in italics means based on the context.

1. The hotel buyers were well *represented* at the convention.

   _____

2. The vice president had several *alternatives*. One was to exhibit at the convention. The other was not to exhibit.

   _____

3. The *regional* sales manager often has to go to the main office.

   _____

4. Let's hope they *procure* several of the items we are selling.

   _____

5. She went to the convention *accompanied* by several of the sales reps.

   _____

Check Yourself

Work Problem

You have just received a telephone call from Jesse Dupree, the Midwest sales representative. He says, "Some of my customers are complaining that they haven't received furniture ordered more than three weeks ago." He points out that normally orders are filled in less than two weeks. He asks what is causing the delay and what he should tell his customers.

You remember that a memo was recently sent to all sales representatives with information about delays in orders. Jesse says he has not seen it. Look at your copy of the memo to see if you can help Jesse.

```
DATE:     November 2, 199—

TO:       All Sales Representatives

FROM:     Al Humphries, Production Manager

SUBJECT:  DELAYS IN PROCESSING ORDERS

It is important that you know that the
production plant is facing a backlog of
work.  We will not be able to fill some
orders as quickly as we usually do.  This
is partly due to an unexpected increase in
business last month.  It has been
exacerbated by some mechanical problems we
have had at the factory.

This month some orders may take up to four
weeks to fill.  Please ask your customers
to bear with us.  We expect to be back to
our usual two-week turnaround by the first
of December.  Christmas sales should not
be affected.


mt
```

Exercise

Try to decide the meaning of difficult words from their context. Choose the best definition for the words and phrases listed below. Choose the meaning of the word closest to that used in the memo.

1. backlog

   a) wood used to make furniture
   b) lack or shortage
   c) buildup
   d) breakdown

2. exacerbated

   a) fixed
   b) made worse
   c) improved
   d) caused

3. bear with us

   a) stop ordering
   b) write to us
   c) help us with deliveries
   d) wait patiently

4. turnaround

   a) look the other way
   b) time between receiving an order and filling it
   c) delay
   d) tone of voice

Now consider your work problem and the memo you are reading. Answer the following questions. Remember to define, plan, read, and check.

What is your purpose for reading this memo?

_____

_____

Why is it taking longer than usual for the plant to ship orders?

_____

_____

How long does Mr. Humphries expect to have delays?

_____

_____

How much time does it usually take of to fill an order?

_____

_____

Answers to Problem-Solving Practice Questions

Define Your Problem

What is my purpose for reading this material?

To find out if this is memo on annual furniture convention.

What should I be able to do when I finish reading?

Know whether or not to put memo on Ms. Smith's desk.

Plan Your Solution

What information do I need from this material to solve my work problem?

Information that tells me who it is from and what it is about.

How carefully will I have to read to find the information I need?

Skim quickly to see if this is the right memo.

Read

What information do the format clues give me?

When it was written. Who received it. Who sent it. What it is about.

What do I already know about this situation that will help me?

It is from Alex Burn. It is about the furniture convention.

Should I continue reading this material?

No. I can see that this is the right memo.

What information is important because it helps me solve my work problem?

Who the memo is from and what it is about.

| Check Your Solution |

Did I accomplish my purpose? (What information did I find?)

Yes. It is from Alex Burns and is about the furniture convention.

Did the information help me solve my work problem? How?

Yes. This is the memo to put on Ms. Smith's desk.

Answers to Skills Practice Exercise A

1. *concentrate* means "look at, focus on"
2. *refer* means "send them, tell them to talk to"
3. *implement* means "do, finish"
4. *correspond* means "match, agree with"
5. *initial* means "first, beginning"

LESSON 2

Reading Forms to Find Information

Many different kinds of *forms* are used in business. Some common forms are invoices (or bills), purchase orders, and mailing labels. Lines and boxes on forms make it easy for a person filling out the form to provide all the needed information. You often do not find whole sentences or paragraphs on forms.

Here is a common invoice, which shows what Comfort Line Furniture Co. bought from Rutledge Stationery:

Who sent the invoice

Where and to whom to send the item purchased

Date the item was shipped

Number that shipping company gives to item

Description of item being shipped

Rutledge Stationery

2323 West Road
St. Paul, MN 55116

INVOICE: 3321

Tel: 612-550-1112
Fax: 612-550-2221

Ship to:	Comfort Line Furniture Co. 567 Sun Highway East Washington, MN 55444		Attn: Carolyn Potter	
Bill to:	Comfort Line Furniture Co. 567 Sun Highway East Washington, MN 55444		Attn: Randy Fuller	
	Date Shipped: 3/18/9-	Ship Via: UPS	Purchase Order No. 10-0410-91	
Item No.	Description	Quantity	Unit Price	Cost
ST349	Felt tip pens	3 doz.	7.00	$21.00
			Subtotal:	$21.00
			Shipping:	.75
			Sales Tax:	1.60
			Total Due:	$23.35

Please enclose yellow copy with payment.

Where and to whom to send the invoice (or bill)

Purchase order number for easy reference

Cost of item being shipped

Total amount owed

Special instructions

How item was shipped.

Amount being shipped

Reading To Find Information

You will use many forms at work to find different kinds of information. The same form, such as an invoice, might look different with different companies. Whatever kind of form you must read, your reading strategy can be the same.

22

Work Problem

You are the assistant to Randy Fuller, office manager for Comfort Line Furniture. Several calculators were bought about a month ago. He has asked you to find out the price for each. Also, he wants to know if he has approved the invoice for payment. The purchase order number is 24-0476-91. There is a folder on your desk labeled "Invoices." Among the many invoices in it, you find the following item:

Elton Office Electronics

INVOICE: 2435

23 Fairview Avenue
St. Paul, MN 55116

Tel: 612-005-2112
Fax: 612-522-1001

Account #: Com924			Date: 7/14/9-	
Bill to: Comfort Line Furniture Co. 567 Sun Highway East Washington, MN 55444			Attn: Randy Fuller	
Ship Rush __ Normal _X_			Purchase Order No. 24-0476-91	
Item No.	Description	Quantity	Unit Price	Cost
134-682	Shredder	1	309.00	$309.00
21-5834	Calculator	2	24.00	48.00
H421-63	Typewriter	2	269.00	538.00
OK for payment *- R.F.*			Subtotal:	$895.00
			Shipping:	
			Sales Tax:	69.00
			Total Due:	$964.00
Please return pink copy with payment.				

Define Your Problem

What is my purpose for reading this material?

To find out if this is the information I need.

What should I be able to do when I finish reading?

Find out the price of the calculators and if Mr. Fuller okayed the invoice.

Plan Your Solution

What information do I need from this material to solve my work problem?

Purchase order number, price, and whether it was approved for payment.

How carefully will I have to read to find the information I need?

I can skim until I find the three pieces of information I need.

Read

What information do the format clues give me?

Parts of the purchase order will help me find what I need.

What do I already know about this situation that will help me?

Purchase order number, items shipped, how the invoice is organized.

Should I continue reading this material?

Only until I've found what I need.

What information is important because it helps me solve my work problem?

Price for each calculator and signature of approval.

| Check Your Solution |

Did I accomplish my purpose? (What information did I find?)

Yes, this is the correct invoice with the information I need.

Did that information help me solve my work problem? How?

Yes. I found the information that Randy Fuller asked me for.

Problem-Solving Practice

Now apply your strategy to another work problem.

Work Problem

Yesterday, Mr. Fuller sent a package to Anna Choo in the San Francisco office of Comfort Line Furniture (2712 Adam Street, San Francisco, CA 94101, 415-782-8100). He sent it by Speedy Express for overnight delivery.

This morning, Ms. Choo calls to say she has not received the package. You have to find out what happened to it. Before calling Speedy Express, you pull your copy of the mailing label from the file to see if it has been filled out correctly.

Sender's Copy   For information call 1-800-555-0000

SPEEDY EXPRESS

Sender's account #: 48-784-22   Package #: 789473829

Sender's address:

```
Randy Fuller
Comfort Line Furniture Company
567 Sun Highway
East Washington, MN 55444
```

Recipient's phone and address:

```
415-555-8100
Anna Choo
Comfort Line Furniture Co.
2712 Adam Street
San Francisco, CA 94101
```

Delivery (check one): Next AM __x__   Next PM ____   2-day ____

Package (check one): Letter __x__   Box ____

Payment: Bill (check one): Sender __x__ Recipient __ Credit card ____

Define Your Problem

What is my purpose for reading this material?

_____

_____

What should I be able to do when I finish reading?

_____

_____

Plan Your Solution

What information do I need from this
material to solve my work problem?

_____

_____

_____

_____

How carefully will I have to read to find
the information I need?

_____

_____

_____

Read

What information do the format clues
give me?

_____

_____

_____

_____

What do I already know about this
situation that will help me?

_____

_____

_____

_____

Should I continue reading this material?

_____

_____

What information is important because
it helps me solve my work problem?

_____

_____

_____

Check Your Solution

Did I accomplish my purpose? (What information did I find?)

_____

_____

_____

_____

Did that information help me solve my work problem? How?

_____

_____

_____

_____

Answers to the Problem-Solving Practice questions are on pages 38-39.

On Your Own

Here are four more work problems. As you work through them, remember to define your purpose and plan your solution. After reading, check to see if you have solved your problem.

Work Problem A

Randy Fuller says that the office is nearly out of #10 envelopes. Some were ordered with many other supplies two weeks ago. Several cartons arrived this morning. He asks you to find the envelopes quickly.

You do not want to waste time opening all the new packages and looking inside them for the envelopes. You go to one that seems the right size. On the outside is a flap that says "packing slip enclosed." You pull out the packing slip to see what it tells you is in the carton.

PACKING SLIP

Rutledge Stationery
2323 West Road, St. Paul, MN 55116

Date Shipped: 9/20/9-　　No: PGL-01472

Ship To:

Comfort Line Furniture Company
567 Sun Highway
East Washington, MN 55444

Quantity: 2500

Description: #10 Envelopes

Weight: 20 lbs
No. of Pkg. in Shipment: 3

What is your purpose for reading this form?

_____

_____

What does the form say is in the carton?

_____

_____

What envelopes are you looking for? Are they in this carton?

_____

_____

What action should you take?

_____

_____

Work Problem B

Mr. Fuller tells you the company is buying stationery from a new source called Bartlett Stationery. He says their first order has just arrived. He asks you to check their invoice to find out what was shipped. He also wants to know what they charge for shipping.

INVOICE from Bartlett

Date: 8/6/9-

Qty	Item	Unit Price	Cost
10	Pens	.75	$7.50
4	Message pads	3.00	12.00
5	Labels	2.00	10.00
		Subtotal:	$29.50
		Shipping Charge:	0
		Tax:	5.50
		Total	$35.00

Note: shipping not charged on orders over $10.00

What is your purpose for reading this form?

_____

_____

What was included in this shipment?

_____

_____

What did Bartlett charge for shipping?

_____

_____

Work Problem C

Randy Fuller ordered several items from Rutledge Stationery. One item was 500 expense account forms and the other was 20 boxes of letterhead stationery. Two cartons from Rutledge Stationery arrived this afternoon.

Mr. Fuller asks you to send the expense account forms to Penny Smith in the marketing department right away. You can send the letterhead stationery to the general supply room later. One of the packing slips looks like this.

PACKING SLIP

Rutledge Stationery
2323 West Road, St. Paul, MN 55116

Date Shipped: 11/2/9-   No: PFW-15035

Consigned to: XYZ Shipping, Powel, MN

Ship To:

Comfort Line Furniture Company
567 Sun Highway
East Washington, MN 55444

Cust. No.: 32998

Quantity: 250

Description: 11x17 Expns Forms

Weight: 15 lbs

No. of Cartons in Shipment: 2

What is your purpose for reading this form?

_____

_____

How does the packing slip help you solve your problem?

_____

_____

What should you do with this carton?

_____

_____

Work Problem D

Mr. Fuller asks you to call Speedy Express Mail Service about a package that was shipped from Comfort Line. It was to Home Furnishings Shop in Cloverdale, Iowa. The floor manager at the Home Furnishings Shop called today to complain that it has not arrived. You pull the sender's copy of the mailing label from the file and check to see if all the information was filled in.

Sender's Copy   For information call 1-800-888-0000

SPEEDY EXPRESS

Sender's account #: 48-784-22   Package Number: 883377000-2

Sender's address:

```
Randy Fuller
Comfort Line Furniture Company
567 Sun Highway
East Washington, MN 55444
```

Recipient's phone and address:

```
515-555-1234
Home Furnishings Shop
718 Hartford Avenue
Springfield, Illinois 62700
```

Delivery (check one): Next AM __x__   Next PM ____   2-day ____

Package (check one): Letter ____   Box __x__

Payment: Bill (check one): Sender __x__ Recipient __ Credit card ____

What is your purpose for reading this form?

_____

_____

Has the mailing label has been filled out correctly? What problem do you find?

_____

_____

What might you do to find out about the package?

_____

_____

Besides the name and address of Home Furnishings Shop, what other information from the mailing label might Speedy Express need to help you find the package?

_____

_____

Skills Practice: Finding a Word's Meaning

Using the context is the best way to find a word's meaning. If that does not work, though, you can try to break the word into parts. Then look at its parts for clues to its meaning. A word can be made up of three parts:

1. The root
2. A beginning part (<u>prefix</u>)
3. An ending part (<u>suffix</u>)

Prefixes and Roots

A prefix is added to the beginning of a word to give it a new meaning.

For example, in the Rutledge Stationery invoice, you saw the word *subtotal*.

Prefix	**(Meaning)**	**Root**
sub-	(under)	total

Subtotal, then, means "under the total" or "less than the total." As you can see on the invoice, a shipping charge and sales tax were added to the subtotal to make the full total.

On the same invoice, you also saw the word *enclose*.

Prefix	**(Meaning)**	**Root**
en-	(in, with)	close

Enclose, then, means "to close in or put in."

In Work Problem C you saw the word *consigned* in the packing slip form.

Prefix	**(Meaning)**	**Root**
con-	(with, together)	sign

Consign means "with sign or mark." To *consign* means "to sign over, to give to."

Exercise A

In each sentence below, the word in italics has a prefix. Identify the prefix and root word. Write them in the space below the sentence. Give their meanings and then the meaning for the full word.

1. The bill is *enclosed* with the shipment.

    prefix:_____   meaning: _____

    root: _____   meaning: _____

    meaning of full word: _____

2. The *subtotal* was only $16, but the shipping charge was $4.

    prefix:_____   meaning: _____

    root: _____   meaning: _____

    meaning of full word: _____

3. The two orders were *conjoined*.

    prefix:_____   meaning: _____

    root: _____   meaning: _____

    meaning of full word: _____

4. Don't forget to fill out the *subsections* of the invoice.

    prefix:_____   meaning: _____

    root: _____   meaning: _____

    meaning of full word: _____

5. What shipping company did you *consign* that shipment to?

    prefix:_____   meaning: _____

    root: _____   meaning: _____

    meaning of full word: _____

Abbreviations and Symbols

An abbreviation is a short form of a word. A symbol is something very short that stands for a longer word. Notice the examples on the list below.

Word	Common Abbreviation or Symbol
shipping	shpg.
invoice	inv.
number	no.
attention	attn.
percent	%
and	&
number	#

Instead of breaking a word down to find its meaning, try to recognize the whole word from the part.

Exercise B

Answer the questions below.

1. What is *No.* as in *Item No.* an abbre-   _____
    viation for?

2. What does # in *account #* and *pack-   _____
    age #* stand for?

3. In the Speedy Express invoice, you saw *Next AM*, and *Next PM*. Which means "next morning" and which means "next afternoon"? _____

4. What does *Cust. No.* mean? _____

Answers to Skills Practice Exercises A and B are on page 40

Exercise C

Answer the questions below.

1. *She enlisted the help of several people in order to do the job quickly.* What does *enlisted* mean?

_____

2. *The manager was subjected to a lot of complaints over the way he handled the argument.* What does *subjected* mean?

_____

3. *The style of the letter conforms to the style the company wants us to use at all times.* What does *conform* mean?

_____

4. What does the abbreviation *No.* mean?

_____

5. You have been told to go to a meeting at 3 *P.M.* What does *P.M.* mean?

_____

Check Yourself

Work Problem

A box of material was sent to Andy Archer at Home Furnishings Outlet. Later in the day a letter, Randy Fuller sent a letter to Archer for delivery the next afternoon. Archer has just called to say the package has not arrived. Mr. Fuller asks you to find out why. This is the sender's copy of a mailing label.

Sender's Copy   For information call 1-800-555-0000
SPEEDY EXPRESS

Sender's account #: 48-784-22   Package Number: 883377000-2

Sender's address:

    Randy Fuller
    Comfort Line Furniture Company
    567 Sun Highway
    East Washington, MN 55444

Recipient's phone and address:

    313-555-8181
    Andy Archer
    Home Furnishings Outlet
    28 River Street
    Detroit, MI 94101

Delivery (check one): Next AM ____   Next PM ____   2-day __x__

Package (check one): Letter ____   Box __x__

Payment: Bill(check one):   Sender __x__   Recipient __   Credit card ____

Exercise

Before solving the work problem, try to determine the meaning of the symbols and abbreviations used in the label above. Circle the letter of the correct meaning.

1. #

    a) Slip
    b) Ticket
    c) Number
    d) Pounds

2. Acct

    a) Action
    b) Account
    c) Accurate
    d) Accountant

3. Tel.

     a) Telephone
     b) Telegraph
     c) Telecommunications
     d) Television

4. Next AM

     a) Night
     b) No special time
     c) Before noon
     d) After noon

5. Next PM

     a) After noon
     b) Night
     c) No special time
     d) Before noon

Now look at your work problem and the form you are reading. Answer the following questions. Remember to define, plan, read, and check.

What is your purpose for reading this form?

_____

_____

Is this the sender's copy for the letter or the box of material?

_____

_____

Is the box to be delivered before the letter or after?

_____

_____

Answers to Problem-Solving Practice Questions

Define Your Problem

What is my purpose for reading this material?

To find out if mailing label provided all information.

What should I be able to do when I finish reading?

Call Speedy Express and ask what happened to package.

Plan Your Solution

What information do I need from this material to solve my work problem?

Address and phone number of San Francisco office; delivery instructions; method of payment.

How carefully will I have to read to find the information I need?

Skim to find all boxes with information I need; read this info to see if correct.

Read

What information do the format clues give me?

Choo's address, phone number, method of payment, time of delivery.

What do I already know about this situation that will help me?

Mailing label format; correct address.

Should I continue reading this material?

No, there is no reason to look at this any further.

What information is important because it helps me solve my work problem?

It is important that I know that all the information on the mailing label was correct.

Check Your Solution

Did I accomplish my purpose? (What information did I find?)

Yes. I found errors on the label.

Did that information help me solve my work problem? How?

Yes. I can now call Speedy Express.

Answers to Skills Practice Exercises

Exercise A

1. prefix: *en-*   meaning : in with
   root: *close*   meaning: shut
   meaning of full word: shut in with
2. prefix: *sub-*   meaning: under
   root: *total*   meaning: all
   meaning of full word: under the or less than the total
3. prefix: *con-*   meaning: with
   root: *joined*   meaning: together
   meaning of full word: together with
4. prefix: *sub-*   meaning: under
   root: *section*   meaning: part
   meaning of full word: part under, lower part
5. prefix: *con-*   meaning: with, together
   root: *sign*   meaning: mark, autograph
   meaning of full word: sign together

Exercise B

1. Number
2. Number
3. AM means next morning, and PM means next afternoon
4. Customer Number

LESSON 3

Reading Charts
and Tables to Find Information

Businesses often use graphics in their written communications. Graphics combine words and symbols to present information. Symbols include bars, lines, and circles.

Look over the following types of charts that you could find in the offices of Leisure Stores, Inc., a chain of stores selling recreational products. You can see that they are designed in different ways. However, they have much in common.

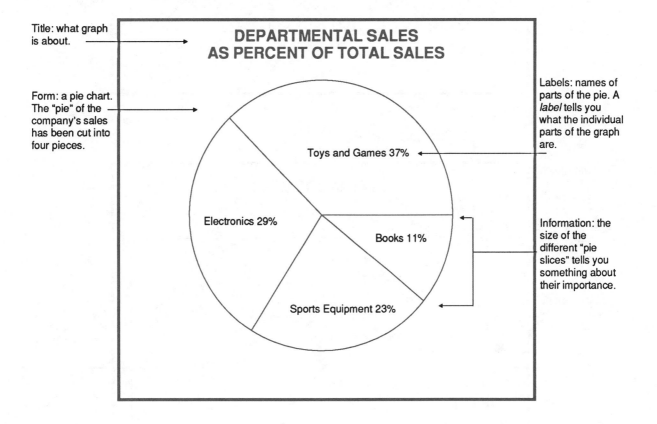

Title: what graph is about.

Form: a pie chart. The "pie" of the company's sales has been cut into four pieces.

DEPARTMENTAL SALES AS PERCENT OF TOTAL SALES

Toys and Games 37%

Electronics 29%

Books 11%

Sports Equipment 23%

Labels: names of parts of the pie. A *label* tells you what the individual parts of the graph are.

Information: the size of the different "pie slices" tells you something about their importance.

41

Title: what graph
is about.

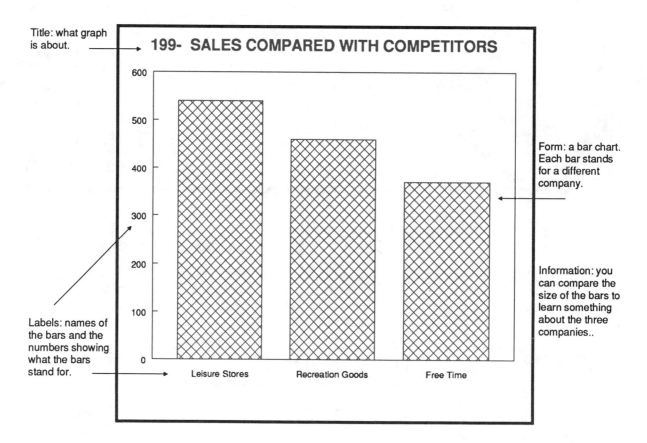

199- SALES COMPARED WITH COMPETITORS

Form: a bar chart.
Each bar stands
for a different
company.

Information: you
can compare the
size of the bars to
learn something
about the three
companies..

Labels: names of
the bars and the
numbers showing
what the bars
stand for.

Title: what graph
is about.

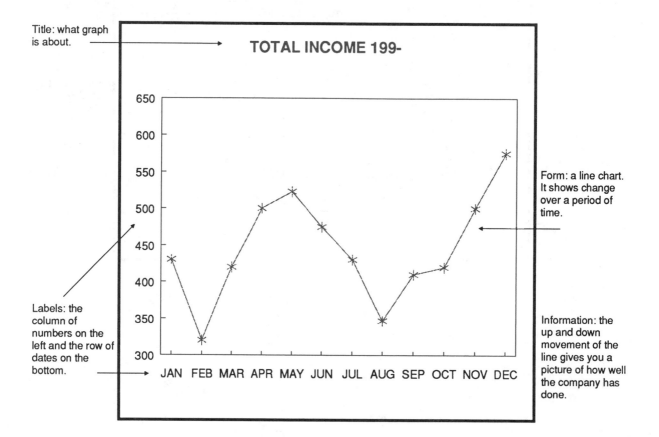

TOTAL INCOME 199-

Form: a line chart.
It shows change
over a period of
time.

Labels: the
column of
numbers on the
left and the row of
dates on the
bottom.

Information: the
up and down
movement of the
line gives you a
picture of how well
the company has
done.

Title: what the table is about.

Labels: names of the columns.

Labels: names of the rows.

Form: a table. Information is given in columns (five) and rows (seven). Each cell or square (where a column meets a row) holds information.

Information: the grid allows you to find a particular fact quickly and easily.

REGIONAL BIMONTHLY SALES BY DEPARTMENT

	Toys & Games	Electronics	Sports	Books
Northeast	35%	32%	19%	14%
Southeast	35%	27%	25%	13%
Midwest	40%	22%	26%	12%
MT States	36%	33%	23%	8%
Southwest	42%	26%	23%	9%
West Coast	41%	27%	21%	11%

Reading To Find Information

Now, look at one of the graphs again and see how Leslie Snow reads it to find information. As a buyer at Leisure Stores, Leslie must know when sales are high or low because she must make decisions about what and when to order. She wants to find out which months had the highest sales last year.

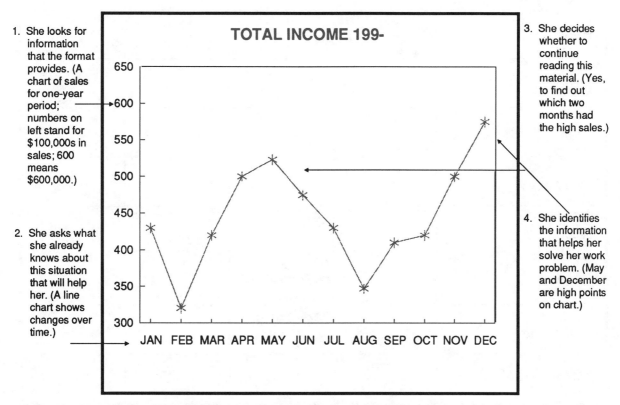

1. She looks for information that the format provides. (A chart of sales for one-year period; numbers on left stand for $100,000s in sales; 600 means $600,000.)

2. She asks what she already knows about this situation that will help her. (A line chart shows changes over time.)

3. She decides whether to continue reading this material. (Yes, to find out which two months had the high sales.)

4. She identifies the information that helps her solve her work problem. (May and December are high points on chart.)

Leslie read to find information in a document. Before taking those steps, she used the problem-solving strategy for reading. Let's go through another work problem using this strategy.

Work Problem

Fred Conti is part of a team of buyers. This team is putting together a list of toys and games that Leisure Stores hopes to make big sellers.

Clyde Morrow calls him to set up a meeting with the toy department to discuss sales strategy. "We need a long meeting, three or four hours. Check your calendar. See what days and times this week would be good for you. Give me several choices. I have to match a lot of different schedules." He adds that he wants the meeting in the morning or afternoon so lunch will not interrupt it.

Week-At-A-Glance

	Mon	Tue	Wed	Thu	Fri
08:00					
09:00	Bimonthly Buyers Meeting		Doctor Appointment		
10:00		Meet with Marketing People			Conference Call to Atlanta office
11:00					
12:00					
01:00					
02:00				Budget Due	
03:00			No Appointments Finish		
04:00			Semiannual Budget ↓		
05:00					

Define Your Problem

What is my purpose for reading this material?

To find times when I am free for a 3 or 4 hour meeting.

What should I be able to do when I finish reading?

Have several different times when I could meet.

Plan Your Solution

What information do I need from this material to solve my work problem?

Blocks of time not already scheduled.

How carefully will I have to read to find the information I need?

Skim to find times for the meeting.

Read

What information do the format clues give me?

Blank space blocks of time. Columns are days. Rows are hours.

What do I already know about this situation that will help me?

It is a calendar that shows things I'm doing.

Should I continue reading this material?

No. I have a morning and three afternoons free.

What information is important because it helps me solve my work problem?

Monday, Tuesday, or Friday afternoon or on Thursday morning would fit my schedule well.

Check Your Solution

Did I accomplish my purpose? (What information did I find?)

Yes. I found four different times that I am free to have the meeting.

Did that information help me solve my work problem? How?

Yes. I gave Mr. Morrow several choices.

Problem-Solving Practice

Now use your strategy on another work problem.

Work Problem

The human resources department for Leisure Stores runs a program for training new sales clerks. It lasts for one 40-hour week. Three kinds of training activities take place. These are classroom instruction, motivational meetings, and on-the-job training.

Al Gomez, your manager, wants to know how much time new clerks spend in on-the-job training during the forty-hour week. The human resources department gives you this chart showing.

NEW EMPLOYEE TRAINING

Motivational Meetings
40% (16 Hours)

Classroom
10% (4 Hours)

On-the-job Training
50% (20 Hours)

Define Your Problem

What is my purpose for reading this
material?

_____

_____

What should I be able to do when I finish reading?

_____

_____

| Plan Your Solution |
_____

What information do I need from this material to solve my work problem?

_____

_____

_____

_____

How carefully will I have to read to find the information I need?

_____

_____

_____

| Read |
_____

What information do the format clues give me?

_____

_____

_____

_____

What do I already know about this situation that will help me?

_____

_____

_____

_____

Should I continue reading this material?

_____

_____

What information is important because it helps me solve my work problem?

_____

_____

_____

_____

| Check Your Solution |

Did I accomplish my purpose? (What information did I find?)

_____

_____

_____

_____

Did that information help me solve my work problem? How?

_____

_____

_____

_____

Answers to the Problem-Solving Practice questions are on pages 59-60.

On Your Own

Here are four more work problems. Remember to define your purpose and plan your solution. Read to find information and then, if you need to, reread some or all of the document carefully. Finally, check to see if you have solved your problem.

| Work Problem A |

Leisure Stores has bought the rights to a new board game. Before selling the game throughout the country, the company wants to test sales in a region where games usually sell well. Carmine Vara gives you the following table. She says, "Take a look at this table and let me know which of the six sales regions would be the best area for testing the new game."

REGIONAL TOY SALES BY TYPE

	Electronic Toys	Educational Toys	Construction Toys	Games
Northeast	12%	15%	21%	16%
Southeast	19%	17%	18%	13%
Midwest	16%	12%	16%	28%
MT States	21%	23%	17%	13%
Southwest	14%	14%	13%	19%
West Coast	18%	19%	15%	11%

What is your purpose for reading this chart?

_____

_____

What are the labels for each row?

_____

_____

What are the labels at the top of each column? Which one must you read?

_____

_____

In what region do games sell well?

_____

_____

Work Problem B

Sales of most products change over time. There are periods when sales are high and periods when they are low. It is important to introduce the new game in a period when game sales are usually high. Carmine Vara gives you the following chart. She asks you to decide which quarter of the year would be the best for putting the new game on the market.

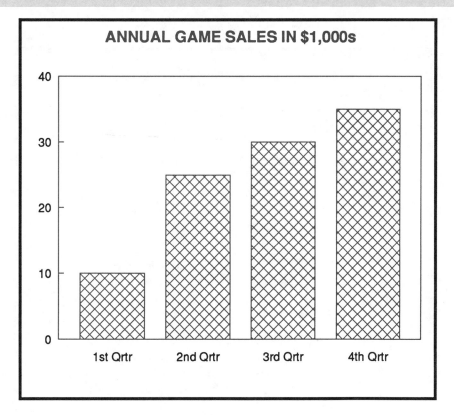

ANNUAL GAME SALES IN $1,000s

What is your purpose for reading this chart?

_____

_____

There are four bars. What period of time does each bar represent?

_____

_____

Which quarter of the year would you recommend the new game be put on sale?

_____

_____

Could you make your recommendation to Ms. Vara if the bars did not have labels? Explain your answer.

_____

_____

Work Problem C

Al Gomez must report on how customers pay for the toys they purchase. Do they pay cash? Do they use the company's thirty-day charge plan? Do they use other credit cards? What cards? The report will help the company set future credit policies. Mr. Gomez gives you the following chart. He asks you to give him the information he needs for his report.

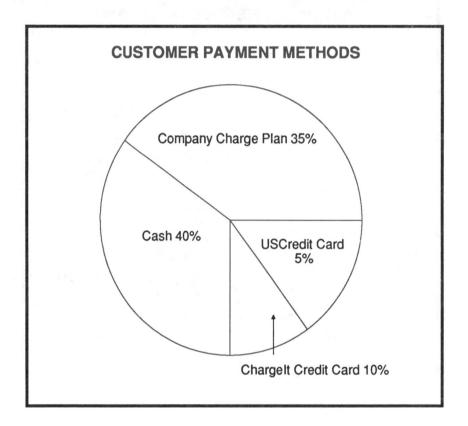

CUSTOMER PAYMENT METHODS

Company Charge Plan 35%

Cash 40%

USCredit Card 5%

ChargeIt Credit Card 10%

What is your purpose for reading this chart?

_____

_____

What method do customers use least to pay for toys at Leisure Stores?

_____

What method do customers use most to pay for toys at Leisure Stores?

_____

_____

Work Problem D

Al Gomez must make sure that he has enough toys and games in stock. To do this, he keeps track of monthly sales of each item. He says, "I'm not sure when is the best time to order playing cards. Find last year's graph showing the sales of playing cards by month. Tell me the two months that sales are highest. Also tell me the lowest month, so I do not order at that time."

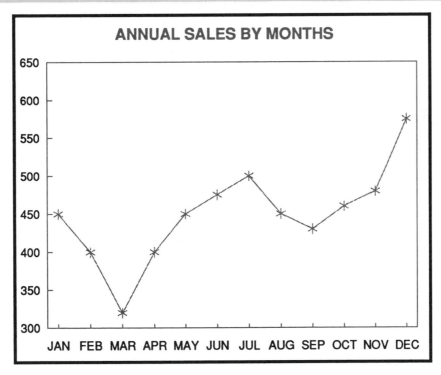

What is your purpose for reading this graph?

_____

_____

What information will this graph give you?

_____

_____

What are the two highest sales months for playing cards?

_____

_____

What is the lowest sales month for playing cards?

_____

_____

Is it necessary to know the exact number of sales to solve your work problem? Why?

_____

_____

Skills Practice: Finding a Word's Meaning

Here are more common prefixes used in business. As you learned in Lesson 2, a prefix is added to the beginning of a root word to give it another meaning. Knowing the prefix or the root word can help you determine what the new word means.

Example: A common root word in business is *port*. A common prefix is *trans-*.

Prefix	**(Meaning)**	**Root**
trans-	(across)	port

Port means "to carry." The word *transport* thus means "to carry across."

Example: In the Week-At-A-Glance calendar, the word *semiannual* appears.

Prefix	**(Meaning)**	**Root**
semi-	(half)	annual

Semi means "half." *Annual* means "yearly." Thus, *semiannual* means "half a year."

Example: The word *bimonthly* appears in the table showing regional sales by department.

Prefix	**(Meaning)**	**Root**
bi-	(two)	month

This word has the prefix *bi* meaning two, the root word *month*, and the suffix *ly*. *Bimonthly* means "every two months."

Example: In the calendar table "Week-At-A-Glance," you saw the word *inter-department*.

Prefix	**(Meaning)**	**Root**
inter-	(between, among)	department

The prefix *inter-* and the root word *department* mean "between departments."

Checking the parts of a word to find its meaning often works. Be careful, though. Not all words that appear to be made up of prefixes, roots, and suffixes really are. A common word you see in business is *invoice*. This is not made up of a prefix *in* and a root word *voice*. Thus, you cannot determine its meaning this way.

Sometimes, the same prefix can mean two different things. Above you read that *bimonthly* means "every two months." *Biweekly* can mean either "every two weeks" or "twice a week." The best test is to make sure the word makes sense in the sentence you are reading.

Exercise A

In each sentence below, identify the prefix and root of the word in italics. Write them in the space below the sentence. Give their meanings and then the meaning for the full word.

1. I have the *biannual* report on sales.

    prefix:_____   meaning: _____

    root: _____   meaning: _____

    meaning of full word: _____

2. Have the bar chart ready for our *semiweekly* meeting.

    prefix:_____   meaning: _____

    root: _____   meaning: _____

    meaning of full word: _____

3. The bar graph shows our *international* sales.

    prefix:_____   meaning: _____

    root: _____   meaning: _____

    meaning of full word: _____

4. I need a line graph that shows *bimonthly* sales.

    prefix:_____   meaning: _____

    root: _____   meaning: _____

    meaning of full word: _____

5. That pie chart is for *interoffice* use.

    prefix:_____   meaning: _____

    root: _____   meaning: _____

    meaning of full word: _____

Answers to Skills Practice Exercise A are on page 60.

Exercise B

Here are five more sentences with words using the common prefixes you have just learned. Write the prefix and root of the words in italics on the line below the sentence. Give their meanings and then the meaning of the full word.

1. That is an *intercity* bus.

    prefix:_____   meaning: _____

    root: _____   meaning: _____

    meaning of full word: _____

2. That worker is only *semiskilled*.

   prefix:_____   meaning: _____

   root: _____   meaning: _____

   meaning of full word: _____

3. We must check the machine *biweekly*.

   prefix:_____   meaning: _____

   root: _____   meaning: _____

   meaning of full word: _____

4. The tasks are *interlocked*.

   prefix:_____   meaning: _____

   root: _____   meaning: _____

   meaning of full word: _____

5. That chart has a *semicircle* in it.

   prefix:_____   meaning: _____

   root: _____   meaning: _____

   meaning of full word: _____

Check Yourself

Work Problem

Leisure Stores has been having a year-long contest to increase sales. Prizes are given to individual salespersons. Also, every salesperson in the department that has the best overall sales record will receive bonuses.

Al Gomez is manager of the toy department. He wants his department to win. Every two months, company officials send out a chart showing the relative sales of each department. Al is away on a conference. He calls and asks you to get the newest sales chart and tell him what it says. Here is the chart.

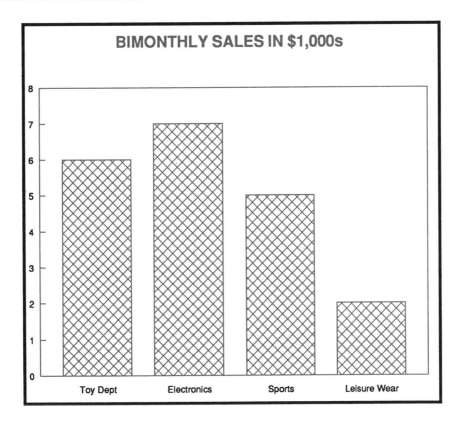

Exercise

As you read, try to decide the meaning of any difficult words from their parts. Consider all the words with prefixes, which are listed below. Write the parts of the word in the correct blank. Give the meaning of the prefix and root word. You may use a dictionary to check your work.

1. interdepartmental

   prefix:_____   meaning _____

   root: _____   meaning _____

2. bimonthly

    prefix:_____   meaning: _____

    root: _____   meaning: _____

3. percentages

    prefix:_____   meaning: _____

    root: _____   meaning: _____

Now consider your work problem and the chart you are reading. Answer the following questions. Remember to define, plan, read, and check.

What is your purpose for reading this chart?

_____

_____

What general information does this document give you?

_____

_____

Which department has the highest sales?

_____

_____

How is the toy department doing compared to the other departments?

_____

_____

Answers to Problem-Solving Practice Questions

Define Your Problem

What is my purpose for reading this material?

To find out hours new clerks spend in job training.

What should I be able to do when I finish reading?

Find information Mr. Gomez wants.

Plan Your Solution

What information do I need from this material to solve my work problem?

How many hours are spent in training.

How carefully will I have to read to find the information I need?

Skim to understand labels. Then read more carefully to find what I need.

Read

What information do the format clues give me?

Size of different pieces of pie show number of training hours.

What do I already know about this situation that will help me?

A pie chart shows how different amounts compare.

Should I continue reading this material?

No.

What information is important because it helps me solve my work problem?

Sizes of pieces in circle (or pie) and specific numbers relating to "training" part of circle.

Check Your Solution

Did I accomplish my purpose? (What information did I find?)

Yes. I found that new clerks spend 20 hours in on-the-job training.

Did that information help me solve my work problem? How?

Yes. I gave Mr. Gomez information he wanted.

Answers to Skills Practice Exercise A

1. *bi-* means "two." *Annual* means "year." *Biannual* means "twice a year."
2. *semi-* means "half." *Week* means "seven days." *Semiweekly* means "twice a week."
3. *inter-* means "among, between." *National* means "a country." *International* means "among nations or countries."
4. *bi-* means "two." *Month* means "30 days." *Bimonthly* means "every two months."
5. *inter-* means "among, between." *Office* means "a place of work." *Interoffice* means "among offices."

LESSON 4

Reading Reference Material to Find Information

You will often use reference materials at work. Reference materials collect large amounts of information in one place. For example, a dictionary is a collection of words with definitions, and an atlas is a collection of maps.

Companies often give their employees a handbook. It contains information on company procedures and rules. It might tell about worker benefits, holidays, and what to do if you are ill. Your office worker's handbook is a useful reference book.

Rick Diaz is a new assistant in the Ace Public Accounting Company. The Ace Office Reference Book is on his desk. The table of contents in it looks like this:

Reference books often start with a list of major sections in the book

Table of Contents

First subsection on telephones

Third subsection on telephones

Fifth subsection on telephones

Reference books often end with an index, which is a detailed alphabetical list of important information in the book.

Reading To Find Information

Now look at the table of contents again and see how Rick reads it.

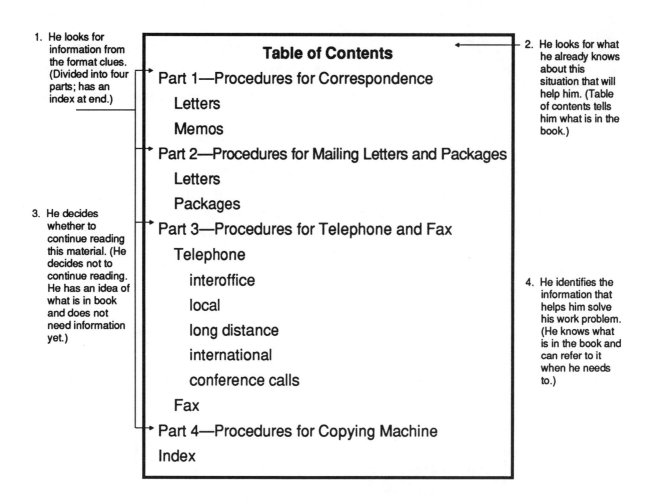

1. He looks for information from the format clues. (Divided into four parts; has an index at end.)

2. He looks for what he already knows about this situation that will help him. (Table of contents tells him what is in the book.)

3. He decides whether to continue reading this material. (He decides not to continue reading. He has an idea of what is in book and does not need information yet.)

4. He identifies the information that helps him solve his work problem. (He knows what is in the book and can refer to it when he needs to.)

Table of Contents

Part 1—Procedures for Correspondence

   Letters

   Memos

Part 2—Procedures for Mailing Letters and Packages

   Letters

   Packages

Part 3—Procedures for Telephone and Fax

   Telephone

     interoffice

     local

     long distance

     international

     conference calls

   Fax

Part 4—Procedures for Copying Machine

Index

Let's go through another work problem using the problem-solving strategy.

Work Problem

You work at Ace for Jane Florio, one of the accountants. Ms. Florio wants you to do some copying for her. You are to make fifty copies of a twenty-five-page report. She will need them next week. She also wants five copies of a new tax form by this afternoon. She gives you a large chart and asks you to make a reduced copy on regular-size paper.

You go to Part 4 of the Ace Manual for information that will help you with Ms. Florio's copying. This is the first page in Part 4:

Part 4—Procedures for Copying Machine

Section A Using office copiers

Area A copier—for regular-size paper and small numbers of copies, see page 34

Area B copier—for special sizes, colored paper, and collating, see pages 35-37

Section B Using outside services—for large quantities, see pages 38-39

Section C Using rush services, see page 39

Define Your Problem

What is my purpose for reading this material?

To find information on copying and to use the info.

What should I be able to do when I finish reading?

Turn to right pages for information I need.

Plan Your Solution

What information do I need from this material to solve my work problem?

How to make a reduced copy. How to get a large quantity of copies.

How carefully will I have to read to find the information I need?

I can skim the first page, then read the other pages for specific information.

Read

What information do the format clues give me?

There are several procedures for making copies at Ace.

What do I already know about this situation that will help me?

Table of contents that tells me what is in the manual. I also know what information I need.

Should I continue reading this material?

Yes. Section A for tax forms and chart. Section B for report.

What information is important because it helps me solve my work problem?

Information on large copies and on large quantities.

| Check Your Solution |

Did I accomplish my purpose? (What information did I find?)

Yes. Information I need is in manual.

Did that information help me solve my work problem? How?

Yes. When I read further, I will solve my work problem.

Problem-Solving Practice

Now use your strategy to solve another work problem.

Work Problem

Ms. Florio asks you to telephone four of her clients. One of them is in the same town. Two of them are in other states. The fourth one is in Paris, France. She also wants you to send a fax message to a fifth client. You get out your Ace Manual and turn to the opening page of Part 3—Procedures for Telephone and Fax. It looks like this:

Part 3—Procedures for Telephone and Fax

Section A Telephone

    interoffice calls, see page 19

    local calls, page 21

    long distance calls, see pages 23-26

        list of area codes, see page 23
        how to dial, see page 24
        time differences, see page 25
        low rates—high rates, see page 26

    international calls, see pages 27-30

        list of country codes, see page 27
        how to dial, see page 28
        time differences, see page 29
        low rates—high rates, see page 30

    conference calls, see pages 31-34

        operator assistance, see page 31
        how to dial, see page 32
        how to plan, see pages 33-34

Section B Fax

    how to prepare cover sheet, see pages 35-36

    how to send, see page 37

    location of fax machines, see page 38

Define Your Problem

What is my purpose for reading this material?

What should I be able to do when I finish reading?

_____

_____

| Plan Your Solution |

What information do I need from this material to solve my work problem?

_____

_____

_____

_____

How carefully will I have to read to find the information I need?

_____

_____

_____

| Read |

What information do the format clues give me?

_____

_____

_____

_____

What do I already know about this situation that will help me?

_____

_____

_____

_____

Should I continue reading this material?

_____

_____

What information is important because
it helps me solve my work problem?   _____

_____

_____

_____

| Check Your Solution | _____

Did I accomplish my purpose? (What
information did I find?)   _____

_____

_____

_____

Did that information help me solve my
work problem? How?   _____

_____

_____

_____

Answers to the Problem-Solving Practice questions are on pages 78-79.

On Your Own

Here are four more work problems using pages from reference material. Remember to define your purpose and plan your solution. Read and, if you need to, reread the page. Finally, check to see if you have solved your problem.

Work Problem A

Ms. Florio asks you to order office supplies. The items she wants are #10 envelopes, adhesive tape, extra-strength rubber bands of various sizes, and file folders. A catalog from Rutledge Stationery and Office Supply Company is on your shelf. It has an index at the back listing all the supplies in the catalog. You look in it to see if you can find the items you need to order.

INDEX

Envelopes
Airmail 45
Clasp 51
Expanding 52
First Class 42
6 Size 40
10 Size 41
Payroll 46
Self-Sealing 48
Waterproof 50
Window 44

File Cabinets
Lateral 120
Mobile 124
Open Shelf 118
Steel 121
Wood 122

File Folders
Alphabetical 59
Card Size 66
Dividers 64
Expanding 67
Hanging 65
Manila 62
Pocket 68
Vinyl 69

Rubber Bands
Regular 135

Tape
Adding Machine 143
Adhesive 145
Magnetic 146
Postage Meter 144

What is your purpose for reading this index?

_____

_____

Will you be able to order the envelopes and tape from this catalog?

_____

_____

What should you do to find out if the catalog has extra-strength rubber bands?

_____

_____

What additional information should you have before you order the file folders?

_____

_____

Work Problem B

Ms. Florio asks you to prepare the agenda for the Tax Accountants Annual Workshop and mail it to the people who will attend. You want to be sure to address people the proper way: Mr., Ms., or Mrs. You need some ideas on preparing the report. You could also use some help using commas. On your shelf is a reference book called *The Style Manual*. You look at the table of contents to see if it will help you.

What is your purpose for reading this table of contents?

_____

_____

What section and page numbers in *The Style Manual* would you see for information on addressing people properly?

_____

_____

What section of the manual explains the use of commas?

_____

_____

Will *The Style Manual* give you the names of the people who will attend the Tax Accountants Annual Workshop?

_____

_____

Work Problem C

No one is happy with the labels used on the file folders. They do not stick or fit the folders. Ms. Florio asks you to see if you can find better labels. In your past job you used a different brand of label that works well. It is made by Bernat Company. The Rutledge catalog has an index of supplies by manufacturer. This index lists companies and the supplies each one makes. You look to see if Rutledge carries Bernat file-folder labels.

INDEX

Arco & Elkhorn Company
Desk Chairs 98
File Cabinets 104, 123-4
Step Stools 145

Allway Publishers
Account Ledgers . . . 32, 35, 37
Expense Books 43
Labels
    File Folders 3-34
    Mailing 82-86

Bernat Company
Glue 12, 42, 51-53

Labels
    File Folders 34-35
    Mailing 81-83
Markers 92
Rubber Cement 50
Tape
    Adhesive 56
    Packing 88

Bick
Dividers 31
File Folders 55
Labels
    Mailing 83, 85-88

What is your purpose for reading this page?

_____

_____

Does Rutledge carry products from Bernat Company in its catalog?

_____

_____

What pages would you see to find information on Bernat Company file-folder labels?

_____

_____

What other Bernat Company products are carried in the Rutledge Catalog?

_____

_____

Work Problem D

Ms. Florio puts you in charge of training part-time workers during the busy season. She tells you not to give them copies of the Ace Office Reference Book. Instead, she says to give them just the pages they need. They must know how to make interoffice and local telephone calls. They must also know how to prepare letters and packages for mailing. They will not send any letters or packages outside the country. You must select the correct pages to copy for them.

Ace Office Reference Book
Table of Contents

Part 1—Procedures for Correspondence

Letters
how to type 2-8
file copies 9-10

Memos
how to type 12-14
file copies 15-16

Part 2—Procedures for Mailing Letters and Packages

Letters
first class 17-18
overnight handling . . . 19-20
international 21-22

Packages
first class 24-25
third class 26-27
overnight handling . . . 28-29
international 30-31

Part 3—Procedures for Telephone and Fax
Telephone
interoffice 33
local 34
long distance 35-37
international 38-39
conference calls . . . 40-43
Fax 44-47

What is your purpose for reading this page?

_____

_____

Which pages will you copy to tell people how to make interoffice phone calls?

_____

_____

Which pages will you copy to tell people how to prepare letters for mailing?

_____

_____

Which pages will you copy to tell people how to mail packages?

_____

_____

Skills Practice: Finding a Word's Meaning

Longer words may be made up of parts. If you do not know the meaning of the long word, its parts may help you. As you have read, the parts are prefix, root, and suffix.

Sometimes a word is made up of two root words. *Laptop* is an example. The two words *lap* and *top* suggest the whole meaning: something small enough to fit on top of a lap. Other common words made up of two separate words are:

airmail	outsized
halfway	overdue
lunchroom	overnight
outlook	overweight
outside	undercharge

You have already learned some prefixes used often in business. Here are some more.

Example: The familiar word *telephone* has two parts:

Prefix	**(Meaning)**	**Root**
tele-	(distance)	phone

Tele means distance. *Phone* means sound. So *telephone* suggests sending sound over a distance, which is what the instrument does.

Example: Earlier in this lesson, you read "How To Prepare Cover Sheet."

Prefix	**(Meaning)**	**Root**
pre-	(before, earlier)	pare

The word *prepare* thus means "to make or have ready."

Example: This lesson is about reference books. The word *reference* has the prefix *re-,* which means *"again."* It has the root *fer,* which means *"carry."*

Prefix	**(Meaning)**	**Root**
re-	(again, back)	fer

The word *reference* means "something that you can go back to again."

Reference also has the suffix *-ence.* Without the suffix, you have *refer. Refer* is an action word: you carry or point back to. Add the suffix *-ence* and you have a word that describes a book.

Exercise A

Look at each word below. On the line, write the word in parts: prefix and root, or two words. Give the meaning of the parts and then the meaning of the whole word. Some of the prefixes you met in earlier lessons.

1. interoffice

    parts: _____   meaning: _____

2. international

    parts: _____   meaning: _____

3. afternoon

    parts: _____   meaning: _____

4. laptop

    parts: _____   meaning: _____

5. waterproof

    parts: _____   meaning: _____

Answers to Skills Practice Exercise A are on page 79.

Exercise B

Here are five more sentences with words using these common prefixes. Write the prefix and root of the words in italics on the line below the sentence. Write their meanings and then the meaning of the full word.

1. The customer *prepaid* this bill.

    prefix:_____   meaning: _____

    root: _____   meaning: _____

    meaning of full word: _____

2. Please *redo* this report.

    prefix:_____   meaning: _____

    root: _____   meaning: _____

    meaning of full word: _____

3. Did you send the *telegram*?

    prefix:_____   meaning: _____

    root: _____   meaning: _____

    meaning of full word: _____

4. Send that in the *overnight* mail.

    prefix:_____   meaning: _____

    root: _____   meaning: _____

    meaning of full word: _____

5. We make *shatterproof* glass.

    prefix:_____   meaning: _____

    root: _____   meaning: _____

    meaning of full word: _____

Check Yourself

Work Problem

Your coworkers are cleaning out files to make room for new projects. Ms. Florio wants you to shred old files before putting them out with the trash. You have to find a company that rents shredders. You look in the yellow pages of the telephone book and find this page.

Rental Service Stores and Yards

Andy's Rent A Tent

Tents for all occasions—weddings, anniversaries, BBQs.
400 Bank 944-1111

Bailey & Standish

Boat rentals—for day trips, overnight, and weekend.
Call for information and rates. 941-4444

Burgess & Holmes

Office Equipment—fax machines, laptop computers, shredders,
and more. 941-0001
(See our ad on page 520.)

Wallace-Kiely Company

Equipment for homeowner & industry—lawn care,
heavy equipment, backhoes, power tools. 944-2200

Exercise

Read the words below. Use slashes (/) to break them into parts. Choose the best meaning from the list below the word.

1. overseas
    a) supervises
    b) on the other side of the ocean
    c) misses
    d) floods

2. backlog
    a) diary
    b) fire wood
    c) something not done
    d) agenda

3. overlook
   a) miss, not see
   b) supervise
   c) see clearly
   d) read

4. shredder
   a) a machine that shreds
   b) a machine that copies
   c) a machine that shades
   d) a machine that shrinks

5. homeowner
   a) someone who owns a home
   b) someone who rents a home
   c) someone who builds a home
   d) someone who wants a home

6. backhoe
   a) a steamshovel
   b) a hoe that digs with backward movement
   c) a rough terrain forklift
   d) an air compressor

Now consider your work problem. Read the information from the yellow pages again and answer the following questions. Remember to define, plan, read, and check.

What is your purpose for reading this page from the telephone book?

_____

_____

What company should you call to rent a shredder?

_____

_____

If you want more information on this company what can you do?

_____

_____

What are two other things you could rent from this company?

_____

_____

Answers to Problem-Solving Practice Questions

Define Your Problem

What is my purpose for reading this material?

To find out if manual has phoning and faxing information.

What should I be able to do when I finish reading?

Find information for making phone calls and sending faxes.

Plan Your Solution

What information do I need from this material to solve my work problem?

Information for making phone calls and sending faxes.

How carefully will I have to read to find the information I need?

Skim this page quickly. Read other pages more carefully.

Read

What information do the format clues give me?

Manual has information on several kinds of phone calls.

What do I already know about this situation that will help me?

The table of contents tells me what is in the manual.

Should I continue reading this material?

Yes. I will need more information.

What information is important because it helps me solve my work problem?

Page 21 - interoffice calls. Page 22 - local calls. 23 - 26 - long distance calls. 27 - 30 - international. 35 - 38 - faxes.

Check Your Solution

Did I accomplish my purpose? (What information did I find?)

Yes. I found that the manual has the information I need on phoning and faxing.

Did that information help me solve my work problem? How?

Yes. When I read the information on pages referred to, I will know how to solve problem.

Answers to Skills Practice Exercise A

1. *inter office*: among offices or from one office to another office.
2. *inter national*: among nations or from one nation to another nation.
3. *after noon*: a time after 12 o'clock noon.
4. *air mail*: mail that goes through the air or is sent in an airplane.
5. *shatter proof*: something that does not break into many pieces easily.

Putting It All Together

The following work problems require that you use much of what you learned in Unit I. As you work through the problems, remember to use the problem-solving strategy.

Work Problem A

You have a summer job at MailMart. This large firm sells clothing and sporting goods across the country. To do so, it sends out thousands of catalogs to people. The catalogs list all the items being sold. MailMart sends a new catalog each season. Many customers send in the purchase orders from the catalog when buying. Almost as many customers call and order over the telephone. MailMart also runs a large store. The store is open 24 hours a day. People come from all over to shop there.

Sales Manager Darcie Turner tells you an important meeting is coming up. The meeting is to approve the items and prices that will be in the next catalog. She says, "I must be sure to put the date and time on my calendar. Could you please find this information? It is in the files somewhere. Oh, let me know who else will be attending."

Use the reading materials on the following pages to answer the following questions.

Which document did you select to read? Why?

_____

_____

What is your purpose for reading this document?

_____

_____

What is the date and time of the meeting Ms. Turner asked about?

_____

_____

Did you have to read the whole document carefully? How much of the document did you need to find the information Ms. Turner needed?

_____

_____

| Work Problem B |

Ms. Turner asks your help with keeping a good customer happy. She says, "Juan Cortez is one of our best customers. He was sent the wrong items on his last two orders. He called and told me he has just sent in a new order. He said if we get this order wrong, we will lose his business."

Ms. Turner asks you to find the order, check what Mr. Cortez is ordering, and tell her. She adds, "Let me know if he has any special instructions."

Use the reading materials on the following pages to answer the following questions.

Which document did you select to read?

_____

_____

What is your purpose for reading this document?

_____

_____

What items has Mr. Cortez ordered?

_____

_____

What special instructions does Mr. Cortez give?

_____

_____

DATE: March 4, 199—

FROM: Israel Rojas, General Manager

TO: All Department Managers

SUBJECT: FALL CATALOG MEETING

This is to notify all department managers of the Fall Catalog Meeting. This is an important meeting to prepare the fall catalog. All managers must attend.

The meeting will be held March 18 beginning at 8:30 a.m. in the conference room. The meeting, as usual, will last all day. Please be sure to mark your calendars.

In addition to the usual items, we will discuss the following new items and prices to be included in the fall catalog. If we all agree, these will go in the catalog.

Item	Price
Crewneck Ragg Sweaters	
Men's Regular Dyed	$29.50
Men's Regular Gray	$25.50
Women's Dyed	$29.50
Women's Gray	$25.50
Shawl Collar Ragg Sweaters	
Men's Regular Dyed	$35.00
Men's Regular Gray	$32.00
Women's Dyed	$35.00
Women's Gray	$32.00
Plaid Shirts	
Men's Regular	$21.50
Men's Tall	$23.00
Women's	$21.00
Stretch Denim Jeans	
Men's	$35.00
Women's	$35.00

Thank you and see you at the meeting.

MAILMART Purchase Order Form

ORDERED BY:

Juan Cortez
1122 High Street
Coventry, RI 02816

GIFT ORDER SHIP TO:

Marc Cortez
3302 Middle Road
East Greenwich, RI 01818

Page	Stock No.	Color	Size	How Many	Description	Amount
33	3028	blue	15 ½	2	Oxford cloth shirt	46.00
33	3029	white	15 ½	4	Oxford cloth shirt	92.00
73	8811			1	Cycling computer	41.00

PAYMENT METHOD:			
CREDIT CARD NO.	_____	Item total	179.00
		Regular shipping free	
AMOUNT ENCLOSED	_____	Express shipping	$8.75
BILL SENDER	_____	TOTAL:	187.75

Special instructions:

As you see, this order must be sent to Marc Cortez, not to me. I want it shipped express service to arrive in time for his birthday. Thank you.

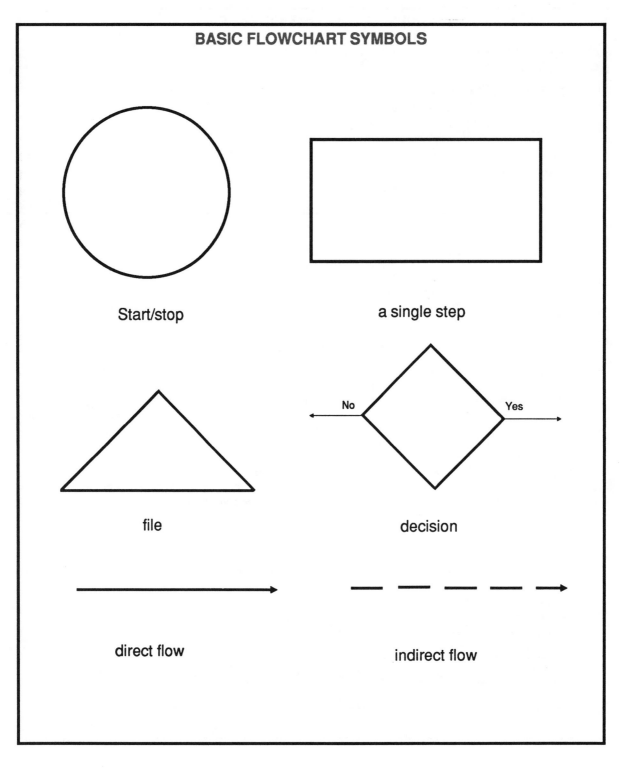

BASIC FLOWCHART SYMBOLS

Start/stop

a single step

file

decision

direct flow

indirect flow

MAILMART COMPANY POLICY MANUAL

Table of Contents

UNIT II

READING TO
FOLLOW DIRECTIONS

Following written directions is an important part of most jobs. Directions may be a short note from your supervisor. Letters, memos, or graphic material could also contain directions for you to follow.

For example, you will often read directions on how to operate business equipment. The written directions for using equipment may be a few words printed on the equipment itself. Or the directions may take up many pages in a manual. You may often need to follow written directions to fill out forms, place phone calls, or order supplies.

In Unit I, you read to find important information. In Unit II, you will read to follow directions. When reading to follow directions, do the following:

1. Look for information that the format provides.

2. Think about what you already know about this situation that will help you.

3. Decide whether to continue reading the material.

4. Pick out the information that helps you solve your work problem.

5. Organize the information to help you carry out the directions.

Coverall Insurance Company

In Unit II, you will work at Coverall Insurance Company. While there you will meet and work with a number of people. Your first boss will be Robert Gaines, manager of the accounting department. You will also work with Samuel Murtz, purchasing manager, and Bertha Hadley, his assistant. One of your coworkers will be Leonard Eto. You will meet Alison Leonard, computer training coordinator, several times. Later you will also work with Alice Roman, sales manager.

Before leaving the unit, you will return to Mailmart for some more experience in the mailorder business. You will work again with Darcie Turner in the sales department.

LESSON 5

Reading Memos to Follow Directions

You have learned that memos are used to pass along information. But they can also be used to give directions. A written memo may take the place of spoken directions or remind you of spoken directions. Your supervisor may tell you how something should be done and then write the directions in a memo. You can then refer to the memo when doing the job.

Reading to Follow Directions

Robert Gaines is manager of the accounting department at Coverall Insurance Company. Notice how he reads a memo to follow instructions.

1. He looks for information from the format clues. (Dated today; from Julia Long in Human Resources Department; about flex-time hours.)

4. He identifies information that is important because it helps him solve his work problem. (Flex-time hours, form that must be filled out, who chooses flex-day, who chooses which day to work late, who approves and signs form.)

DATE: June 5, 199-

TO: Robert Gaines, Acctg Dept.

FROM: Julia Long, Human Resources

SUBJECT: SUMMER FLEX-TIME HOURS

Flex-time hours are 8:00 a.m. to 4:30 p.m. for nine days, with the tenth day off. This day (flex-day) is chosen by the employee, with the supervisor's permission.

Employees must say on Form F-3 the day they will take as their flex-day. This must be the same day each time. For example, employee A might choose Monday of the first week, and employee B Wednesday of the second week.

Because flex-time results in a net loss of 45 working minutes in each two-week period, employees must stay late one day to make up this time. This day is set by the supervisor and applies to everyone in that department.

Supervisor must initial forms before forwarding them to me via interoffice mail.

---

2. He looks for what he already knows about this situation that will help him. (He knew the company was preparing to set up special summer hours.)

3. He decides whether to continue reading this material. (Yes, to be sure he and his employees are following directions.)

5. He organizes the information to help him carry out the directions. (Get Form F-3, decide day to take, set long day, inform people in department, sign form, return it.)

As you can see, the first four steps Robert Gaines follows are the same as those used when reading to find information. The fifth step is new and important. Manuals usually give directions in a step-by-step form, which makes them easy to follow. Directions in memos might not be given this way. You must organize the directions to decide how to carry them out.

Before doing his reading, Mr. Gaines used the problem-solving strategy. Let's go through another work problem using this strategy.

Work Problem

You work in the accounting department of the Coverall Insurance Company. Sometimes Robert Gaines asks you and several coworkers to work late. Mr. Gaines brings you the following memo. He asks you to read it and pass the information to your coworkers. Mr. Gaines stresses the importance of following the directions in the memo.

DATE: June 17, 199-

TO: All Employees

FROM: Albert Janus, Security

SUBJECT: BUILDING SECURITY

At 5:30, building doors are locked by security. Employees working late have unlocked those doors when leaving and have not relocked them. As a result, nonemployees have entered the building. Several items have been stolen, including an expensive laptop computer.

We are instituting new rules for employees leaving the building after 5:30. Employees may no longer exit through a door that has been locked. Three doors to the building will remain unlocked from the inside until 6:30: the north entrance door on level one, the east entrance door on level two, and the door leading to the top level of the parking garage. You may exit by these doors, but you will not be able to reenter through them. They have been fitted with a self-locking mechanism.

Employees leaving the building after 6:30 p.m. must call security at ext. 274 for an escort.

Define Your Problem

What is my purpose for reading this material?

Find out overtime procedures and pass info to coworkers.

What should I be able to do when I finish reading?

Know which doors to use after 5:30 and after 6:30 p.m.

Plan Your Solution

What information do I need from this material to solve my work problem?

Specific steps to follow when working overtime.

How carefully will I have to read to find the information I need?

Carefully, because I sometimes leave the building after 5:30.

Read

What information do the format clues give me?

Written today to all employees who work overtime. From Albert Janus, head of security. About overtime and building security.

What do I already know about this situation that will help me?

Mr. Janus was serious about following directions. It's about security and must be important.

Should I continue reading this material?

Yes. I must know what to do and tell my coworkers.

What information is important because it helps me solve my work problem?

The specific steps for leaving the building after 5:30 and after 6:30.

Did I organize the information to carry out the directions?

Yes.

Check Your Solution

Did I accomplish my purpose? (Was I able to carry out the directions?)

Yes. I know what to do to leave the building after 5:30 and after 6:30.

Did the information help me solve my work problem? How?

Yes. I can follow these directions to avoid more theft. I can pass on these instructions to coworkers.

Problem-Solving Practice

Now apply your strategy to another work problem.

Work Problem

The end of the fiscal year is always a busy time for the accounting department. This year it is even busier because the department is changing to a new computer accounting system. All employees must be trained to use the new system.

Mr. Gaines is busy closing out the company books for the year, so he asks you to take charge of the training schedule. He gives you this memo and asks you to follow its directions.

DATE: July 2, 199-

TO: Robert Gaines, Accounting

FROM: Alison Leonard,
         Training Coordinator

SUBJECT: COMPUTER TRAINING

To schedule the people in your department for computer training, I need some information. I need to know who is experienced on computers and who is a beginner. Do any of your employees have experience with the new software we will be using? Please make a list of their names, phone numbers, and level of experience.

Also, you must decide who should be trained first. Some people may need to use this new program on a daily basis, others only now and then. Please send me a list of the people in your department beginning with those who should be trained first.

Finally, please let me know the first day that you can spare these people for an hour-long introductory (first) session. I'd like to begin training next week.

Define Your Problem

What is my purpose for reading this material?

_____

_____

What should I be able to do when I finish reading?

_____

_____

Plan Your Solution

What information do I need from this material to solve my work problem?

_____

_____

_____

_____

How carefully will I have to read to find the information I need?

_____

_____

_____

Read

What information do the format clues give me?

_____

_____

_____

_____

What do I already know about this situation that will help me?

_____

_____

_____

Should I continue reading this material? _____

_____

What information is important because
it helps me solve my work problem? _____

_____

_____

_____

Did I organize the information to carry
out the directions? _____

_____

_____

| Check Your Solution |

Did I accomplish my purpose? (Was I
able to carry out the directions?) _____

_____

_____

_____

Did the information help me solve my
work problem? How? _____

_____

_____

_____

Answers to the Problem-Solving Practice questions are on pages 104-106.

On Your Own

Now you will read four more memos to follow directions. Remember to define your purpose and plan your solution. Read and, if you need to, reread again carefully. Finally, check to see if you have solved your problem.

Work Problem A

Your company is organizing a quality improvement program called "Quality Counts." Mr. Gaines asks you to be the department's Quality Counts coordinator. He hands you a packet of Quality Counts materials and the following memo.

```
DATE:      September 11, 199-

TO:        Robert Gaines, Accounting

FROM:      Julia Long, Human Resources

SUBJECT:   QUALITY COUNTS PROGRAM

Here are the materials for our company's
Quality Counts program.  Mr. Bennet wants
each manager to assign one employee to be
department coordinator.

The program kick-off is September 15.  The
materials your coordinator will need are in
the packet.  Before September 15, have the
coordinator post the Quality Counts poster
in a central place.  This will raise
employee interest.

When employees arrive for work on the 15th,
they will find their Quality Counts pocket
calendar, button, suggestion forms, and
award booklets.  The September goal poster
will be posted with this month's goal
written in.  It is your job to see that this
is done.

As employees make suggestions, the
coordinator will list their names on the goal
poster throughout the month.
```

What is your purpose for reading this memo?

_____

_____

What directions must you follow before September 15?

_____

_____

What will you give to each employee on September 15?

_____

_____

Is your job finished on September 15? What else must you do?

_____

_____

Work Problem B

The department secretary is on vacation. Mr. Gaines asks you to perform some of his duties while he is away. One of your jobs is to file documents relating to insurance policies. You are unfamiliar with the filing system and the steps to take when filing. The secretary has left you the following memo.

DATE: September 23, 199-

TO: Your Name

FROM: Don Reynolds

SUBJECT: FILING PROCEDURES

Files are in three sections: by alphabet, by number, and by subject. Information concerning insurance policies is filed numerically by policy number. It is cross-referenced alphabetically by the name of the insured person.

File at least once a day. First, underline the policy number on the original paper in black ink. Then, photocopy the policy and underline the name of the insured person in red ink on the photocopy. This photocopy is your cross-reference.

When you have completed these steps for each document, sort them into two stacks: originals and photocopies. File originals by number. File photocopies by alphabet. Arrange each stack in numeric or alphabetic order, and then file the papers.

What is your purpose for reading this memo?

_____

_____

What is the first step you will take when filing?

_____

_____

What is the second step you will take?

_____

_____

What is the last thing you will do before placing the papers in the file?

_____

_____

Work Problem C

Computer training in your department has been completed, but there is some confusion about procedures. People are losing important information because they are not following the correct steps when turning their computers on and off. Alison Leonard sends the following memo to your department. You and all employees are expected to follow the instructions.

```
DATE:      September 29, 199-

TO:        Accounting Department Employees

FROM:      Alison Leonard, Training Coordinator

SUBJECT:   COMPUTER PROCEDURES

Time and information are being lost because
employees are not following correct
procedures when using the computers.

Please follow these steps when turning your
computer on:
Insert your work disk after the computer has
prompted you to type in the date and time.
After inserting disk, always answer "yes"
to the prompt to inspect disk for viruses.
Compare the files on your disk with the
files on the hard drive.  They should be
identical.  If they are not, use the steps
you learned in training to copy the most
recent files onto your disk.  These are the
files you will work on.

When you finish work for the day, follow
these steps:
Save your work on the hard drive and on your
work disk.
Do not shut the computer off while in the
accounting program.
Return to the main menu before shutting the
computer off.

Please call me (ext. 998) if you have
problems.
```

What is your purpose for reading this memo?

_____

_____

What steps will you take after turning your computer on?

_____

_____

What will you do if your work disk and the computer hard drive have different copies of the same file?

_____

_____

What steps will you take before turning your computer off?

_____

_____

Work Problem D

Your company has hired a purchasing manager. In the past, each department purchased its own supplies. Now there will be one program under the direction of purchasing manager Samuel Murtz. You are asked to take charge of setting up the new program in your department. Mr. Gaines asks you to explain the new procedures to the staff at a short meeting this afternoon.

DATE: October 2, 199-

TO: Your Name

FROM: Samuel Murtz, Purchasing Manager

SUBJECT: NEW PURCHASING PROCEDURES
          EFFECTIVE OCTOBER 3

All purchases from every department must be approved by me or my assistant, Bertha Hadley. Your department will receive a supply of requisition forms. Each form is numbered and each section is color-coded.

When your department needs supplies or equipment, complete Form A, the pink requisition form, and send it to me. If you have a supplier, please indicate this on the form. Do not detach this paper from the rest of the five-part form. I will return it to you within five days, marked "approved" or "denied."

If your request is approved, complete forms B through E and distribute them: Form B (white) to the supplier; Form C (blue) to the purchasing department; Form D (yellow) for your files. Form E (gold) is to be attached to the bill and sent to the accounting department after the purchase arrives.

This new system will result in considerable savings. I realize it may also take time and cause some initial delays. Please do not wait until the last minute when ordering. We will be instituting rush procedures in the near future, but they will be for emergency situations only. It is your job to see that your department does not run out of supplies.

What is your purpose for reading this memo?

_____

_____

What is the first thing you do when your department needs supplies?

_____

_____

When do you separate the five-part form? Where does the gold part go?

_____

_____

What are your duties as purchasing coordinator?

_____

_____

Skills Practice: Finding a Word's Meaning

As you learned in Unit I, you can often tell a word's meaning from the sentence and paragraph in which it is found.

Example: In the memo from Samuel Murtz, you read this sentence:

> I realize it may also take time and cause some *initial* delays.

You are probably familiar with the word *initials*, meaning the first letters of your name. In this sentence, the word has a somewhat different meaning. From the context, you can probably determine that it means "first" or "early."

Example: In the memo from Julia Long, you read this:

> Because the flex-time schedule results in a *net* loss of 45 working minutes in each two-week period, employees must stay late one day to make up this time.

The small word *net* could be confusing. Does it have the same meaning as *net* in the phrase *fish net*? No, the context does not support that meaning. The context supports the idea of the *total* loss of minutes during the period. *Net* is another word for "total."

Exercise

Read the following sentences. On the blank lines following each one, write what the word in italics means based on the context. Then write another sentence using the word.

1. Because of this, we are *instituting* new regulations for employees leaving the building after 5:30.

   _____

   _____

2. The end of the *fiscal* year is always a busy time for the accounting department.

   _____

   _____

3. Information *concerning* insurance policies is filed by the policy number and *cross-referenced* by the name of the insured person.

   _____

   _____

4. Insert your work disk after the computer has *prompted* you to type in the correct date and time.

   _____

   _____

5. We will be instituting rush *procedures* in the near future.

   _____

   _____

Answers to Skills Practice Exercise are on page 106.

Check Yourself

Work Problem

When Mr. Gaines asked you to oversee the working of the new purchasing procedures, you expected a few problems. A few people are grumbling and complaining. You start to wonder if it is your fault and if it is only happening in your department. Then you receive the following memo.

DATE: October 15, 199-

TO: Your Name

FROM: Samuel Murtz, Purchasing Manager

SUBJECT: PURCHASING PROCEDURE UPDATE

I have heard that the new purchasing procedures are meeting with some resistance. I expected that there would be a few problems as we implemented the new program. Any new procedure is bound to meet stumbling blocks. However, the overall success of the system validates it.

That does not mean there are no problems. I am asking coordinators to find which steps are working well and which are causing problems. Please list them and any suggestions you may have to improve the process.

I also want you to make an inventory of all supplies your department keeps on hand. I am looking at the possibility of keeping a central supply storage area for all departments.

Exercise

As you read, try to determine the meaning of any difficult words you find from the sentence or paragraph in which you find them. For the words listed below, circle the letter of the one with a meaning closest to the one that is used in the memo.

1. resistance

    a) approval
    b) problems
    c) opposition
    d) variations

2. implement

    a) tool
    b) carry out
    c) destroy
    d) encounter

3. validate

    a) deny
    b) solidify
    c) confirm
    d) address

4. inventory

    a) photograph
    b) itemized list
    c) directory
    d) invitation

Now consider your work problem and the memo you are reading. Answer the following questions. Remember to define, plan, read, and check.

What is your purpose for reading this memo?

_____

_____

What is the first direction you must follow?

_____

_____

After reading this memo, what will you do second?

_____

_____

What is the final step you must take?

_____

_____

Answers to Problem-Solving Practice Questions

Define Your Problem

What is my purpose for reading this material?

Learn details of computer training program.

What should I be able to do when I finish reading?

Follow Alison Leonard's directions and give her information.

Plan Your Solution

What information do I need from this material to solve my work problem?

What to do so my department can be scheduled for computer training.

How carefully will I have to read to find the information I need?

Very carefully, to be sure that I know all the steps to take.

Read

What information do the format clues give me?

Written today to Robert Gaines. From computer training coordinator. About computer training.

What do I already know about this situation that will help me?

May already know something about the new computer program.

Should I continue reading this material?

Yes, I must follow its directions.

What information is important because it helps me solve my work problem?

All the directions, so I can oversee the scheduling of the training.

Did I organize the information to carry out the directions?

Yes.

Check Your Solution

Did I accomplish my purpose? (Was I able to carry out the directions?)

Yes. I know what steps to follow to give Ms. Leonard the information she needs.

Did the information help me solve my work problem? How?

Yes. I now know what is involved in getting computer training scheduled for my department.

Answers to Skills Practice Exercise

1. beginning
2. financial
3. relating to; filed in two places and so marked
4. cued, suggested
5. policies, rules

LESSON 6

Reading Forms to Follow Directions

In Unit I, you learned to read forms to find information. In the office, you will also need to read forms to follow directions. It is important to read forms carefully for directions before you fill them out. Forms are designed to include any information that might be needed. For example, if you do not read directions on an order form, an order may take longer than necessary to be filled.

Person and firm ordering.

1

| Person Ordering: |
| Firm Name: |
| Street Address: |
| City, State, ZIP Code: |

Choices of payment.

PAYMENT OPTIONS:

- [ ] Check or money order enclosed.
- [ ] Bill me later.
- [ ] Please open an account for us.

2

BILL TO:

| Attention: |
| Firm Name: |
| Street Address: |
| City, State, ZIP Code: |

Fill out if the bill is to be sent to a different person or address from those in block 1.

3

SHIP TO:

| Recipient Name: |
| Firm Name: |
| Street Address: |
| City, State, ZIP Code: |

Fill out if the items are to be delivered to another person or address.

What is ordered and amounts.

4

ORDER INFORMATION:

Product Number	Quantity	Description	Size	Unit Price	Totals
			SUBTOTAL:		
			TAX:		
			TOTAL AMOUNT DUE:		

What to print on item ordered.

5

IMPRINT INFORMATION: Send printed sample or fill in wording below.

Reading to Follow Directions

Bertha Hadley is assistant to the manager in the purchasing department of Coverall Insurance Company. She must fill out the form. Notice how she reads it.

1	Person Ordering:	**2** **BILL TO:**
	Firm Name:	Attention:
	Street Address:	Firm Name:
	City, State, ZIP Code:	Street Address:
		City, State, ZIP Code:

PAYMENT OPTIONS:

☐ Check or money order enclosed.

☐ Bill me later.

☐ Please open an account for us.

3 **SHIP TO:**

Recipient Name:

Firm Name:

Street Address:

City, State, ZIP Code:

4 **ORDER INFORMATION:**

Product Number	Quantity	Description	Size	Unit Price	Totals
			SUBTOTAL:		
			TAX:		
			TOTAL AMOUNT DUE:		

5 **IMPRINT INFORMATION:** Send printed sample or fill in wording below.

1. She looks for information from the format clues. (How to fill out the order form.)

2. She looks for what she already knows about this situation that will help her. (She knows what items are wanted.)

3. She decides whether to continue reading this material. (Yes, to understand the directions in each block.)

4. She identifies the information that is important because it helps her solve her work problem. (All of the information is important since it helps to make sure she receives what she wants.)

5. She organizes the information to help her carry out the directions. (She begins filling out form on first line in block 1 and continues in order.)

You have seen how Bertha Hadley read to follow directions on a form. Before reading, she used the problem-solving strategy. Let's go through another work problem using this strategy.

Work Problem

Samuel Murtz is purchasing manager at Coverall Insurance. He has hired you to help Bertha Hadley, his assistant.

Your first assignment is to fill out the order blank below. You are to order 3,000 single window envelopes, 9 1/2" x 4 1/8" (product number 0915). The cost of the envelopes is $108.50. The envelopes must be imprinted with the company's name and mailing address:
  - Coverall Insurance Company
  - P.O. Box 245
  - Stoughton, MA 02070

They must be delivered to Mr. Murtz at the company street address, 2415 Old Hatfield Road. The bill should be sent to Rosalie Donovan at the company's mailing address.

1
Person Ordering:
Firm Name:
Street Address:
City, State, ZIP Code:

2 **BILL TO:**
Attention:
Firm Name:
Street Address:
City, State, ZIP Code:

PAYMENT OPTIONS:

☐ Check or money order enclosed.
☐ Bill me later.
☐ Please open an account for us.

3 **SHIP TO:**
Recipient Name:
Firm Name:
Street Address:
City, State, ZIP Code:

4 **ORDER INFORMATION:**

Product Number	Quantity	Description	Size	Unit Price	Totals
			SUBTOTAL:		
			TAX:		
			TOTAL AMOUNT DUE:		

5 **IMPRINT INFORMATION:** Send printed sample or fill in wording below.

Define Your Problem

What is my purpose for reading this material?

To learn to fill out the order form accurately.

What should I be able to do when I finish reading?

Order correct product with completed form.

Plan Your Solution

What information do I need from this material to solve my work problem?

How to fill out sections of form so that I will receive correct envelopes.

How carefully will I have to read to find the information I need?

Skim form. Then read each section carefully as I fill it out.

Read

What information do the format clues give me?

Each section has specific instructions.

What do I already know about this situation that will help me?

The form requires certain information: what I want, how many, and so on.

Should I continue reading this material?

I can stop reading once I have completed all sections.

What information is important because it helps me solve my work problem?

The directions in each section help me fill in the information

Did I organize the information to carry out the directions?

Yes, and the form's organization helped.

Check Your Solution

Did I accomplish my purpose? (Was I able to carry out the directions?)

Yes. I put the correct information in each section.

Did the information help me solve my work problem? How?

Yes. I ordered the right envelopes with imprint, delivered to Mr. Murtz, billed to Ms. Donovan.

Problem-Solving Practice

Now apply your strategy to another work problem.

Work Problem

You are working as an electrician's assistant. You answer a complaint about a problem in the purchasing department at the Coverall Insurance Company. The problem is a bad wall outlet, and you make the repair. The bill is $150. Mr. Murtz says to bill the company. When you are finished, you must fill out the invoice below and make sure to give the right copies to the right people.

REPAIR INVOICE

Date: 4/3/199–

Customer Name and Address:

```
Coverall Insurance Company
P.O. Box 245
Stoughton, MA 02070
```

Service Performed:

Appliance Repair:_____Electrical Work:_____

Appliance Installation:_____Parts:_____

Total Charge:_____

Method of Payment: Cash:____Check:____Charge:____

White Copy—Customer; Blue Copy—Electrical Company; Pink Copy—Electrician's Records

---

Define Your Problem

What is my purpose for reading this material?

_____

_____

What should I be able to do when I finish reading?

_____

_____

Plan Your Solution

What information do I need from this
material to solve my work problem?

_____

_____

_____

_____

How carefully will I have to read to find
the information I need?

_____

_____

_____

Read

What information do the format clues
give me?

_____

_____

_____

_____

What do I already know about this
situation that will help me?

_____

_____

_____

_____

Should I continue reading this material?

_____

_____

What information is important because it helps me solve my work problem?

_____

_____

_____

_____

Did I organize the information to carry out the directions?

_____

_____

_____

Check Your Solution

Did I accomplish my purpose? (Was I able to carry out the directions?)

_____

_____

_____

_____

Did the information help me solve my work problem? How?

_____

_____

_____

_____

Answers to the Problem-Solving Practice questions are on pages 124-126.

On Your Own

Now you will read four more business forms. Remember to define your purpose and plan your solution. Read and, if you need to, reread some or all of the forms carefully. Finally, check to see if you have solved your problem.

Work Problem A

Today is your first day on the job at Coverall Insurance Company. After discussing your employment, Carla Burk asks you to fill out a W-4 form. The W-4 form tells an employer how much money to take out of your pay for taxes. First you must fill out the Personal Allowances Worksheet. Read the directions on this form to be sure you know how to fill it out.

Personal Allowances Worksheet For 199-, the value of your personal exemption(s) is reduced if your income is over $100,000 ($150,000 if married filing jointly, $125 if head of household, or $75,000 if married filing separately). Get Pub. 919 for details.

A Enter "1" for **yourself** if no one else can claim you as a dependent . . . . **A**_____

B Enter "1" if:
   1. You are single and have only one job; or
   2. You are married, have only one job, and your spouse does not work; or . . . . **B**_____
   3. Your wages from second job or spouse's wages (or the total) are $1,000 or less.

C Enter "1" for your **spouse.** But, you may choose to enter "0" if you are married and have either a working spouse or more than one job (this may help you avoid too little tax withheld) . . . . **C**_____

D Enter number of **dependents** (other than your spouse or yourself) whom you will claim on your return **D**_____

E Enter "1" if you will file as **head of household** on your tax return (see conditions above) . . . . . . **E**_____

F Enter "1" if you have at least $1,500 of **child or dependent care expenses** for which you claim a credit **F**_____

G Add lines A through F and enter total here . . . . **G**_____

For accuracy, do all worksheets that apply.
- If you plan to **itemize or claim adjustments to income** and want to reduce your withholding, see the Deductions and Adjustments Worksheet on page 2.
- If you are **single** and have **more than one job** and your combined earnings from all jobs exceed $27,000 OR if you are **married** and have a **working spouse or more than one job**, and the combined earnings from all jobs exceed $46,000, see the Two-Earner/Two-Job Worksheet on page 2 if you want to avoid having too little tax withheld.
- If **neither** of the above situations applies, **stop here** and enter the number from line G on line 4 of Form W-4 below.

What is your purpose for reading this form?

_____

_____

What other worksheets must you fill out?

_____

_____

After reading this form, do you have any clues about what you will do with the information next?

_____

_____

What information goes on line G?

_____

_____

Work Problem B

Now Ms. Berkley asks you to fill out the W-4 form. Carefully read the directions on the form.

Form **W-4**	**Employee's Withholding Allowance Certificate**	OMB No. 1545-0010
Department of the Treasury Internal Revenue Service	▶ For Privacy Act and Paperwork Reduction Act Notice, see reverse.	**19**

1 Type or print your first name and middle initial   Last name   **2** Your social security number

Home address (number and street or rural route)

City or town, state, and ZIP code

3 Marital status { ☐ Single   ☐ Married   ☐ Married, but withhold at higher Single rate.

Note: *If married, but legally separated, or spouse is a nonresident alien, check the Single box.*

4 Total number of allowances you are claiming (from line G above or from the Worksheets on back if they apply) . . . **4** ____

5 Additional amount, if any, you want deducted from each pay . . . . **5** $ ____

6 I claim exemption from withholding and I certify that I meet **ALL** of the following conditions for exemption:
- Last year I had a right to a refund of **ALL** Federal income tax withheld because I had **NO** tax liability; **AND**
- This year I expect a refund of **ALL** Federal income tax withheld because I expect to have **NO** tax liability; **AND**
- This year if my income exceeds $550 and includes nonwage income, another person cannot claim me as a dependent.

If you meet all of the above conditions, enter the year effective and "EXEMPT" here . . . . . ▶ **6** 19

7 Are you a full-time student? (**Note:** *Full-time students are not automatically exempt.*) . . . . **7** ☐ Yes ☐ No

Under penalties of perjury, I certify that I am entitled to the number of withholding allowances claimed on this certificate or entitled to claim exempt status.

Employee's signature ▶   **Date** ▶ , 19

8 Employer's name and address (**Employer:** Complete 8 and 10 **only if sending to IRS**)   **9** Office code (optional)   **10** Employer identification number

What is your purpose for reading this form?

_____

_____

What will you hand to your employer when you are finished? Who keeps the Personal Allowances Worksheet?

_____

_____

Who will fill out lines 8, 9, and 10?

_____

_____

Do you think you might have to fill out a form like this again if you stay at Coverall Insurance Company? What might change your answers or the amount of money taken out of your paycheck?

_____

_____

Work Problem C

Bertha Hadley asks you to check the order of pens that arrived. You look at the pens and see that your company's name is spelled incorrectly.

The box contains twenty-five dozen pens with the inscription "Cover All Insurance Company" rather than "Coverall Insurance Company." You examine the invoice carefully to see if it includes the Perfect Pen Company's return policy. If it does, you will follow the directions and return the pens.

Perfect Pen Company

3232 South Road
Toledo, OH 43600

SHIPPING INVOICE 9465

Tel: 419-552-2221
Fax: 419-552-1112

Ship to: Coverall Insurance Company
2415 Old Hatfield Road
Stoughton, Mass. 02070

Attn: Bertha Hadley

Bill to: Coverall Insurance Company
P.O. Box 245
Stoughton, Mass. 02072

Attn: Robert Gaines

Date Shipped:
10/12/199-

Purchase
Order No:
345-7890

Item No.	Description	Quantity	Unit Price	Totals
23-794	black felt tip pens	25 dozen	$4/doz.	$100

SPECIAL INSTRUCTIONS:
Inscribe pens: "Coverall Insurance
Company: We Care About You"

Subtotal:	$100
Shipping:	
Sales Tax:	$6.98
Total Due:	$106.98

Terms: Due and payable upon receipt

Return Policy: Returns accepted within 30 days if accompanied by yellow copy of this invoice. Return for like goods only—no cash refunds. To return by mail, call 1-800-555-3321 for package return number and mailing label.

What is your purpose for reading this form?

_____

_____

What information from the invoice will help you solve your problem?

_____

_____

What will you do before mailing the package?

_____

_____

What must you include with the package?

_____

_____

| Work Problem D |

Mr. Murtz and Ms. Hadley will be away from the office attending a meeting. This will be your first time on your own. You ask Ms. Hadley what you should tell people who phone. She says, "Just take a message, and tell them that Mr. Murtz or I will get back to them. Please be sure to take a complete message. Use the telephone message forms, and fill out all the information."

After they leave, the phone rings. Mr. Bennet, the company president, has called a manager's meeting for 9:00 A.M. tomorrow. Mr. Murtz must present a report on the new purchasing program. Mr. Bennet wants to preview the report before the meeting. He asks that Mr. Murtz call him at extension 1432 as soon as he returns. He says it is urgent.

```
┌─────────────────────────────────────────┐
│  For  _____   │
│  Date _____  Time _____         │
│         WHILE YOU WERE OUT                │
│  M  _____    │
│  From _____    │
│  Phone No. _____    │
│            Area Code  Number   Extension  │
├──────────────────────┬────────────────────┤
│ TELEPHONED           │ URGENT             │
├──────────────────────┼────────────────────┤
│ PLEASE CALL          │ WANTS TO SEE YOU   │
├──────────────────────┼────────────────────┤
│ WILL CALL AGAIN      │ CAME TO SEE YOU    │
├──────────────────────┴────────────────────┤
│          RETURNED YOUR CALL                │
├────────────────────────────────────────────┤
│  Message _____  │
│  _____ │
│  _____ │
│  _____ │
│  _____ │
│  _____ │
│                    Operator                 │
└────────────────────────────────────────────┘
```

What is your purpose for reading this form?

_____

_____

What information do you put on the very first line of the form?

_____

_____

Where does the name of the caller go?

_____

_____

What boxes do you check on the form?

_____

_____

Where should you put your name?

_____

_____

Skills Practice: Finding a Word's Meaning

You have learned that the best way to find a word's meaning is to use clues from the sentence or paragraph it is in. However, forms often do not give those types of clues. When reading forms, you will often need to break a word down into its parts.

In Unit I, you learned some common word parts you might find in business writing. Here are some more you should know.

Prefix	**(Meaning)**	**Root**
with-	(away, against)	hold

Example: The W-4 form includes the word *withholding*.

Withholding means "keep away from."

The company *withholds* (keeps away from you) part of your pay for taxes.

Prefix	**(Meaning)**	**Root**
trans-	(across, over)	port

Example: *Transport* is commonly used in business. *Transport* means "to carry" or "send across a distance."

How will you *transport* the goods?

Suffix	**(Meaning)**	**Root**
-able, -ible	(capable of)	apply

Example: The order form at the beginning of this lesson includes the word *applicable*. "We are required to charge you sales tax where *applicable*" means "where sales tax is applied."

Suffix	**(Meaning)**	**Root**
-ize	(to make)	item

Example: In the W-4 worksheet, you read the word *itemize*.

If you plan to *itemize* . . . see page 2.

To *itemize* means "to make a list of items."

Root	**(Meaning)**
duct	(direct, lead)

Example: The root *duct* is common in business. You will often find it joined with the prefix *con-* meaning "with" or "together."

Will you *conduct* the meeting?

Conduct means "to lead or direct together."

Exercise A

In each sentence below, the word in italics has a prefix you will find in business. Identify the prefix and root word. Write them in the space below the sentence. Give their meanings and then the meaning for the full word.

1. Extra charges will apply if your goods are *transported* by air freight.

   prefix:_____   meaning: _____

   root: _____   meaning: _____

   meaning of full word: _____

2. We are *withholding* payment because the shipment was damaged.

   prefix:_____   meaning: _____

   root: _____   meaning: _____

   meaning of full word: _____

3. *Postdated* checks will not be accepted.

   prefix:_____   meaning: _____

   root: _____   meaning: _____

   meaning of full word: _____

4. We *transferred* some of our workers to the new office.

   prefix:_____   meaning: _____

   root: _____   meaning: _____

   meaning of full word: _____

5. Please *conduct* yourself with dignity when you are a representative of this firm.

   prefix:_____   meaning: _____

   root: _____   meaning: _____

   meaning of full word: _____

Answers to Skills Practice Exercise A are on page 126.

Exercise B

Look at the word in italics in each sentence. Write the parts of the word below the sentence. If the word does not have a prefix or suffix, write "none" in the blank. Some of the words are made up of parts you learned in other lessons. Give the meaning of the parts and the whole word. Check your meaning to see if it makes sense in the sentence.

1. Is that a *portable* computer?

   prefix:_____   meaning: _____

   suffix:_____   meaning: _____

   root: _____   meaning: _____

   meaning of full word: _____

2. I *withdrew* the money from the bank.

    prefix:_____   meaning: _____

    suffix:_____   meaning: _____

    root: _____   meaning: _____

    meaning of full word: _____

3. You must *refile* that form.

    prefix:_____   meaning: _____

    suffix:_____   meaning: _____

    root: _____   meaning: _____

    meaning of full word: _____

4. Do not *withhold* information from customers.

    prefix:_____   meaning: _____

    suffix:_____   meaning: _____

    root: _____   meaning: _____

    meaning of full word: _____

5. We *realized* big savings last month.

    prefix:_____   meaning: _____

    suffix:_____   meaning: _____

    root: _____   meaning: _____

    meaning of full word: _____

Check Yourself

Work Problem

You want to change your withholding allowances so that less money is taken from your paycheck for taxes. The human resources department secretary gives you the following Deductions and Allowances Worksheet to fill out.

Deductions and Adjustments Worksheet

Note: *Use this worksheet only if you plan to itemize deductions or claim adjustments to income on your 199- tax return.*

1   Enter an estimate of your 199- itemized deductions. These include: qualifying home mortgage interest, charitable contributions, state and local taxes (but not sales taxes), medical expenses in excess of 7.5% of your income, and miscellaneous deductions. . . . .   **1** $ _____

2   Enter: $5,700 if married filing jointly or qualifying widow(er)
$5,000 if head of household . . . .
$3,400 if single
$2,850 if married filing separately   **2** $ _____

3   **Subtract** line 2 from line 1. If line 2 is greater than line 1, enter zero . . . .   **3** $ _____

4   Enter estimate of your 199- adjustments to income. Include alimony and deductible IRA contributions   **4** $ _____

5   **Add** lines 3 and 4 and enter the total . . . .   **5** $ _____

6   Enter an estimate of your 199- nonwage income (such as dividends or interest income) . . . .   **6** $ _____

7   **Subtract** line 6 from line 5. Enter the result, but not less than zero. . . . .   **7** $ _____

8   **Divide** the amount on line 7 by $2,000 and enter the result here. Drop any fraction.   **8** $ _____

9   Enter the number from Personal Allowances Worksheet, line G, on page 1. . . . .   **9** $ _____

10   **Add** lines 8 and 9. Enter total here. If you use the Two-Earner/Two-Job Worksheet, also enter total on line 1, below. Otherwise, **stop here** and enter this total on Form W-4, line 4 on page 1 . . .   **10** $ _____

Exercise

As you read, try to decide the meaning of any difficult words you find from their parts. Consider the words with prefixes or suffixes listed below. Write the parts of each word in the blank. Then give the meaning of the word. You may refer to a dictionary to check your work.

    1. deduction

        prefix:_____   meaning: _____

        suffix:_____   meaning: _____

        root: _____   meaning: _____

        meaning of full word: _____

    2. adjustments

        prefix:_____   meaning: _____

        suffix:_____   meaning: _____

        root: _____   meaning: _____

        meaning of full word: _____

3. charitable

prefix:_____   meaning: _____

suffix:_____   meaning: _____

root: _____   meaning: _____

meaning of full word: _____

4. nonwage

prefix:_____   meaning: _____

suffix:_____   meaning: _____

root: _____   meaning: _____

meaning of full word: _____

Now consider your work problem and the form you are reading. Answer the following questions. Remember to define, plan, read, and check.

What is your purpose for reading this form?

_____

_____

How does the format help you read the directions?

_____

_____

What is the first thing the directions ask you to enter?

_____

_____

What does the form tell you to do with your final total?

_____

_____

Answers to Problem-Solving Practice Questions

Define Your Problem

What is my purpose for reading this material?

To fill out invoice and give a copy to customer.

What should I be able to do when I finish reading?

Know which copies go to firm, customer, my records.

Plan Your Solution

What information do I need from this
material to solve my work problem?

I will know how to distribute the copies of the repair receipt.

How carefully will I have to read to find
the information I need?

I can skim the form until I find information listed at the bottom.

Read

What information do the format clues
give me?

I must fill out the information requested before I distribute the copies.

What do I already know about this
situation that will help me?

I know what work I have done.

Should I continue reading this material?

No. Stop once I decide where copies should go.

What information is important because it helps me solve my work problem?

The information about which copy goes to the customer.

Did I organize the information to carry out the directions?

Yes.

Check Your Solution

Did I accomplish my purpose? (Was I able to carry out the directions?)

Yes. I filled out the form and distributed copies as directed.

Did the information help me solve my work problem? How?

Yes. I gave out the copies correctly.

Answers to Skills Practice Exercise A

1. prefix: *trans-* means "across," root *port* means "carry," *transported* means "carried across."
2. prefix: *with-* means "away," root *hold* means "keep," *withholding* means "keep away from."
3. prefix: *post-* means "after," root *date* means "the time of a transaction," *postdated* means "to date after the time of a transaction."
4. prefix: *trans-* means "across," root *fer* means "carry," *transfer* means "to carry across, move."
5. prefix *con-* means "together," root *duct* means "lead," *conduct* means "to lead together."

LESSON 7

Reading Tables and Charts to Follow Directions

Graphics such as maps, charts, and tables give directions well. They help readers see the tasks they must perform. Directions that might take several pages of words to explain can often be shown in much less space.

Graphics sometimes contain both a graphic and step-by-step written instructions. The graphic makes the written instructions clear.

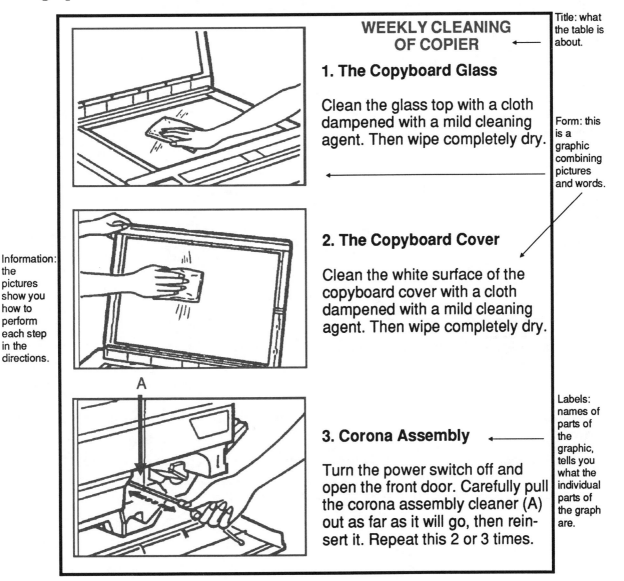

WEEKLY CLEANING OF COPIER ← Title: what the table is about.

1. The Copyboard Glass

Clean the glass top with a cloth dampened with a mild cleaning agent. Then wipe completely dry.

Form: this is a graphic combining pictures and words.

2. The Copyboard Cover

Clean the white surface of the copyboard cover with a cloth dampened with a mild cleaning agent. Then wipe completely dry.

Information: the pictures show you how to perform each step in the directions.

3. Corona Assembly ←

Turn the power switch off and open the front door. Carefully pull the corona assembly cleaner (A) out as far as it will go, then reinsert it. Repeat this 2 or 3 times.

Labels: names of parts of the graphic, tells you what the individual parts of the graph are.

127

Reading to Follow Directions

Now look at this graphic again and see how Leonard Eto reads it to follow directions.

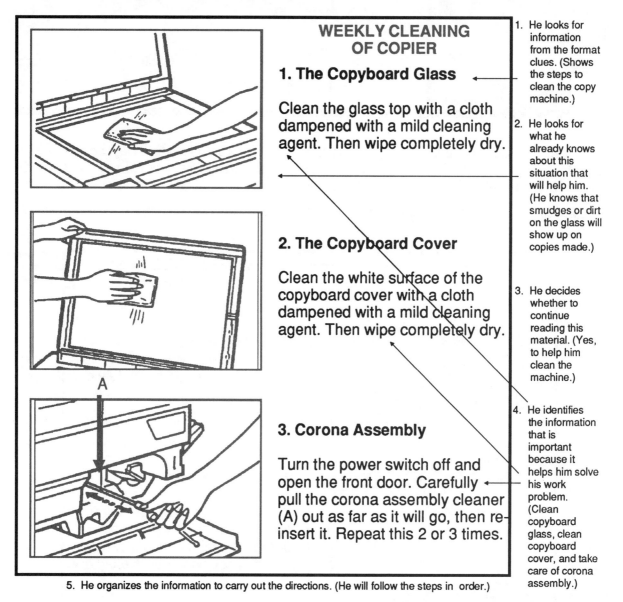

WEEKLY CLEANING OF COPIER

1. The Copyboard Glass

Clean the glass top with a cloth dampened with a mild cleaning agent. Then wipe completely dry.

2. The Copyboard Cover

Clean the white surface of the copyboard cover with a cloth dampened with a mild cleaning agent. Then wipe completely dry.

3. Corona Assembly

Turn the power switch off and open the front door. Carefully pull the corona assembly cleaner (A) out as far as it will go, then re-insert it. Repeat this 2 or 3 times.

1. He looks for information from the format clues. (Shows the steps to clean the copy machine.)

2. He looks for what he already knows about this situation that will help him. (He knows that smudges or dirt on the glass will show up on copies made.)

3. He decides whether to continue reading this material. (Yes, to help him clean the machine.)

4. He identifies the information that is important because it helps him solve his work problem. (Clean copyboard glass, clean copyboard cover, and take care of corona assembly.)

5. He organizes the information to carry out the directions. (He will follow the steps in order.)

You have seen how Leonard Eto read to follow directions using graphics. Let's go through another work problem using the problem-solving strategy.

One of the most common types of charts used to give directions is a flowchart. When given a task, you can discover what to do by reading a flowchart. A flowchart can also help you see where your task fits in relationship to other tasks.

Work Problem

You are responsible for arriving first at Coverall Insurance Company each morning and preparing the office for the day. Leonard Eto gives you this flowchart that he made when this task was his. He suggests that you follow the directions on this chart each morning.

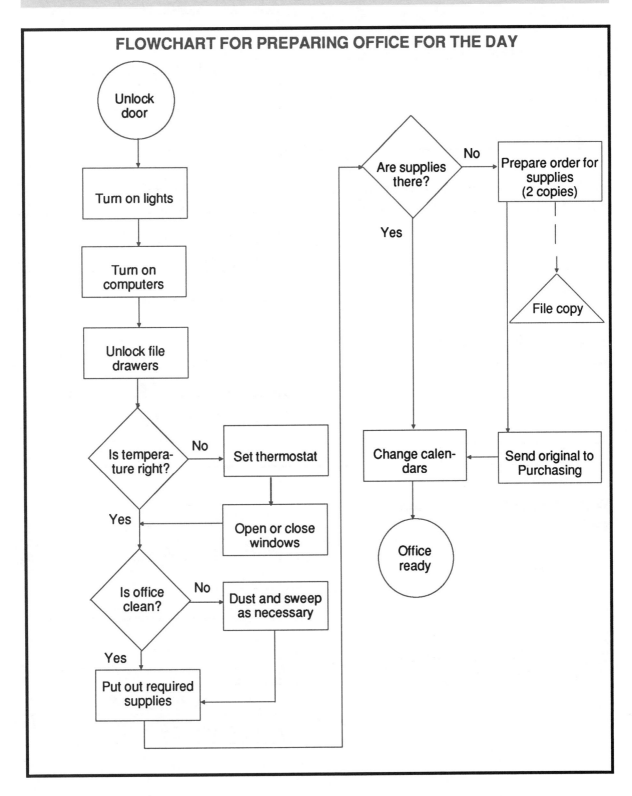

FLOWCHART FOR PREPARING OFFICE FOR THE DAY

Define Your Problem

What is my purpose for reading this material?

Find directions for preparing the office each morning.

What should I be able to do when I finish reading?

Follow procedures in correct order.

Plan Your Solution

What information do I need from this material to solve my work problem?

How to get office ready for the workday.

How carefully will I have to read to find the information I need?

Follow chart and answer questions, then read appropriate answers.

Read

What information do the format clues give me?

Circles, boxes, and arrows.

What do I already know about this situation that will help me?

I'm familiar with the office, which helps me understand the flow chart.

Should I continue reading this material? _Yes, until I have read every step._

What information is important because it helps me solve my work problem? _The information following each arrow._

Did I organize the information to carry out the directions? _Yes._

Check Your Solution

Did I accomplish my purpose? (Was I able to carry out the directions?) _Yes. I know what to do each morning._

Did the information help me solve my work problem? How? _Yes, by charting directions for me to follow._

Problem-Solving Practice

Now apply your strategy to another work problem.

Work Problem

Leonard Eto turned the copy machine on, but the copier did not start. He asks you to fix it, if possible. The chart shown below is posted on the wall above the copy machine. You must decide whether to call the copier repair service.

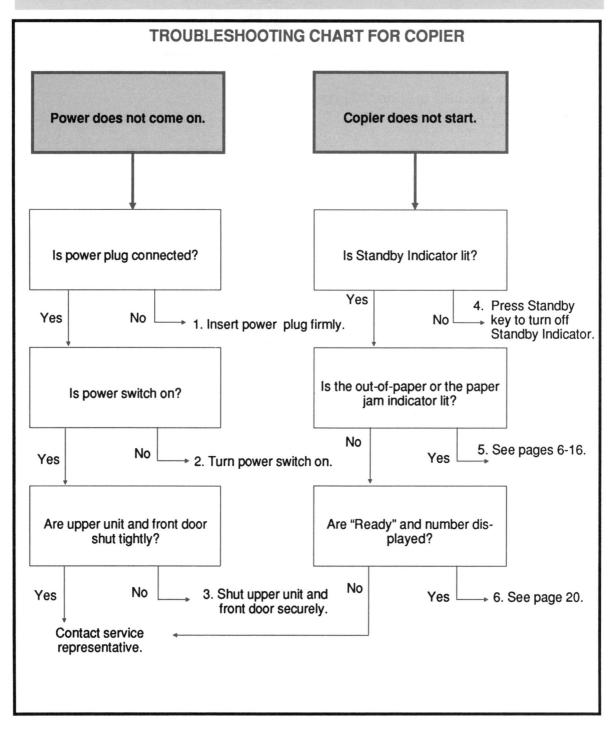

TROUBLESHOOTING CHART FOR COPIER

| Power does not come on. | Copier does not start. |

Is power plug connected?

Yes   No → 1. Insert power plug firmly.

Is power switch on?

Yes   No → 2. Turn power switch on.

Are upper unit and front door shut tightly?

Yes   No → 3. Shut upper unit and front door securely.

Contact service representative.

Is Standby Indicator lit?

Yes   No → 4. Press Standby key to turn off Standby Indicator.

Is the out-of-paper or the paper jam indicator lit?

No   Yes → 5. See pages 6-16.

Are "Ready" and number displayed?

No   Yes → 6. See page 20.

Define Your Problem

What is my purpose for reading this
material?

_____

_____

What should I be able to do when I finish
reading?

_____

_____

Plan Your Solution

What information do I need from this
material to solve my work problem?

_____

_____

_____

_____

How carefully will I have to read to find
the information I need?

_____

_____

_____

Read

What information do the format clues
give me?

_____

_____

_____

_____

What do I already know about this
situation that will help me?

_____

_____

_____

Should I continue reading this material?   _____

_____

What information is important because
it helps me solve my work problem?   _____

_____

_____

_____

Did I organize the information to carry
out the directions?   _____

_____

_____

Check Your Solution

Did I accomplish my purpose? (Was I
able to carry out the directions?)   _____

_____

_____

_____

Did the information help me solve my
work problem? How?   _____

_____

_____

_____

Answers to the Problem-Solving Practice questions are on pages 146-148.

On Your Own

Now you will read four more business charts and graphs to follow directions. Remember to define your purpose and plan your solution. Read and, if you need to, reread some or all of the material carefully. Finally, check to see if you have solved your problem.

Work Problem A

You must mail packets of insurance information and boxes of brochures to insurance agents throughout the country. Leonard Eto gives you the flyer below as a guide. It combines words and pictures to explain the mailing suggestions.

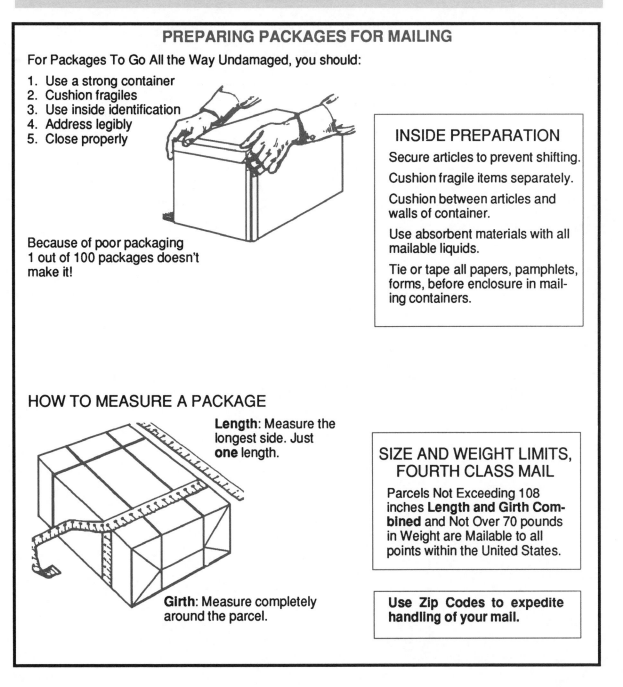

PREPARING PACKAGES FOR MAILING

For Packages To Go All the Way Undamaged, you should:

1. Use a strong container
2. Cushion fragiles
3. Use inside identification
4. Address legibly
5. Close properly

Because of poor packaging 1 out of 100 packages doesn't make it!

INSIDE PREPARATION

Secure articles to prevent shifting.

Cushion fragile items separately.

Cushion between articles and walls of container.

Use absorbent materials with all mailable liquids.

Tie or tape all papers, pamphlets, forms, before enclosure in mailing containers.

HOW TO MEASURE A PACKAGE

Length: Measure the longest side. Just **one** length.

Girth: Measure completely around the parcel.

SIZE AND WEIGHT LIMITS, FOURTH CLASS MAIL

Parcels Not Exceeding 108 inches **Length and Girth Combined** and Not Over 70 pounds in Weight are Mailable to all points within the United States.

Use Zip Codes to expedite handling of your mail.

What is your purpose for reading this page?

_____

_____

What directions must you follow to pack items for mailing?

_____

_____

How do you measure a parcel post package?

_____

_____

What directions should you follow to make sure that your packages arrive safely?

_____

_____

Work Problem B

Sales manager Alice Roman puts you in charge of the department's files. You must see that the correct records are filed. You must also keep the files up-to-date by removing old records.

The company has filing guidelines. They tell you what records to keep, how long to keep them, and where to keep them. The flowchart below will help you keep the department's files in order.

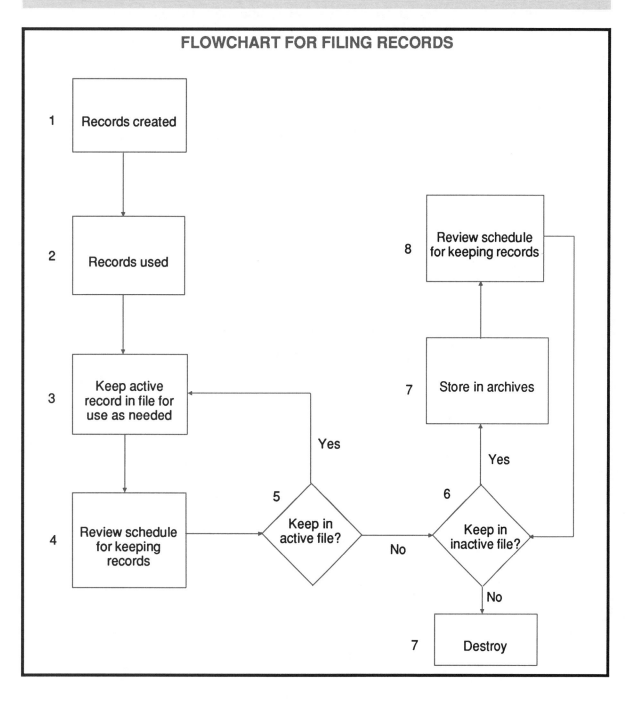

FLOWCHART FOR FILING RECORDS

1 Records created

2 Records used

3 Keep active record in file for use as needed

4 Review schedule for keeping records

5 Keep in active file?

6 Keep in inactive file?

7 Store in archives

7 Destroy

8 Review schedule for keeping records

What is your purpose for reading this chart?

_____

_____

When will you first look at your filing guidelines? When will you next look at them?

_____

_____

What step do you go to if the answer is "yes" at Step 5? What does that next step ask you to do?

_____

_____

What do you do with the record if the answer is "no" at Step 6?

_____

_____

Work Problem C

A new fuel saver thermostat has been put in your office. The temperature display will not come on when you arrive at work one morning. Your supervisor asks you to look up the chart below showing what to do when there is a problem. He says, "See if you can find the problem before you call the maintenance department."

WHAT TO DO WHEN THERMOSTAT DOES NOT WORK

If you cannot solve the problem, call maintenance department

SYMPTOM	CHECK	ACTION
Display is scrambled or flashes 12:00 A and 1.	if program has been entered.	Press BEGIN OFFSET key. If no program, set one up by following programming instructions, page 10.
	battery power.	Remove thermostat from wallplate or subbase, and see Battery Replacement, page 27.
Display will not come on.	mounting of thermostat to subbase or wallplate.	Remove thermostat and reinstall on the subbase or wallplate, making sure case is firmly latched to subbase or wallplate.
	spring finger contacts on back of thermostat.	Remove thermostat from wallplate or subbase. If contact is deformed, rebend to 45-degree angle.
	tightness of current link screws.	Tighten firmly.
	limit switch continuity.	If limit switch is open and room temperature below 94 F (34 C), replace subbase or wallplate.
	CAUTION Next step requires an ac voltmeter and knowledge of how to use it.	
	voltage at wallplace or subbase terminals.	15-30 Vac must be present between R and W terminals. If present, thermostat electronics are defective. Replace thermostat.
Dwelling does not return to comfort temperature at programmed time; i.e., at the end of energy savings period.	offset program stop time. Press END OFFSET.	Reset END OFFSET time for one-half hour earlier. Continue to reset until system is at comfort temperature by desired time.
	A/P indicator on clock display and time-of-day.	Reset clock for correct time.
Temperature offset occurs at the wrong times.	start and stop times by pressing BEGIN OFFSET and END OFFSET keys.	If necessary, reset program to desired start and stop times. Check A/P indicator. Make sure Night and Day programs don't overlap.

What is your purpose for reading this chart?

_____

_____

What are the titles of the chart's columns? What is in each column?

_____

_____

How many possible problems should you check before calling the maintenance department?

_____

_____

What equipment will you ask the maintenance department to bring?

_____

_____

Work Problem D

Leonard Eto is now the manager of Coverall Insurance Company's three southeastern branch offices. He asks you to find the routes that employees of the three offices would use to leave the area if there were a nuclear emergency. You are to type up the correct directions. The offices are in New London, Montville, and East Lyme. The information you need is found on the map in the yellow pages of the telephone book.

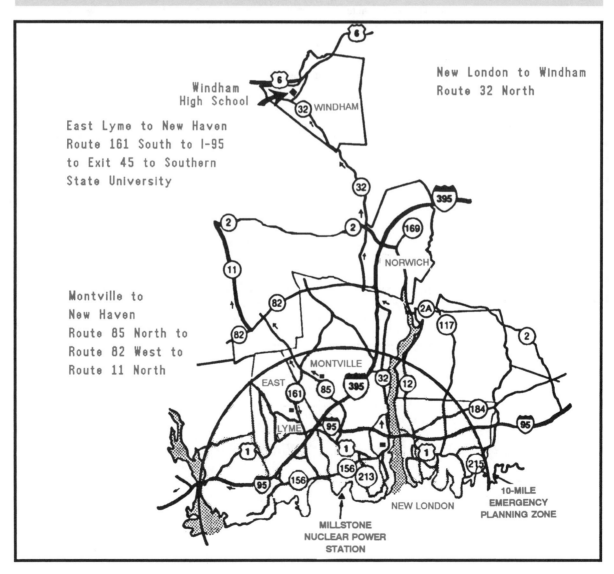

What is your purpose for reading this map?

_____

_____

What directions will you give employees of the New London office?

_____

_____

What directions will you give employees of the East Lyme office?

_____

_____

What directions will you give employees of the Montville office?

_____

_____

Skills Practice: Finding a Word's Meaning

Charts, tables, and graphs are used to explain difficult ideas. They may have difficult words and phrases. If you cannot decide a word's meaning from its context, you must use your skills at breaking words into their parts: prefixes, suffixes, and roots.

Here are more prefixes and root words you should know:

Prefix	(Meaning)	Root
de-	(down, from)	posit
		duct

The prefix *de-* is one of the most common ones. Here are two samples of it.

> You *deposit* money into a bank account.

The root *posit* means "to place."

> At work, some money is *deducted* from your paycheck.

The root *duct* means "to take."

Consider this sentence:

> The company *depreciates* its equipment over time for tax purposes.

The word in italics is long. If you look at its parts, its meaning might be clear. The root is *preciate*. This might make you think of a more familiar word: *appreciate*, which has another prefix *ap-*. Appreciate means "to favor or improve." The prefix *de-* gives the word an opposite meaning.

To *depreciate* means "the equipment becomes worth less money over time."

Prefix	(Meaning)	Root
ex-	(out of, from)	ped

In the instructions for mailing packages, you read the word *expedite*. The root word is *ped*, meaning "foot." The prefix *ex-* suggests moving the foot out of or from a place. With these clues and the context, you might be able to guess that *expedite* means to move along or do something quickly.

Prefix	(Meaning)	Root
un-	(reverse, not)	avail

> The clerk told me that item was *unavailable*.

If you did not know the word, you could probably decide that the item you asked for is not in the store. Using word part clues and the context can often help you arrive at a word's meaning.

Exercise

Look at the word in italics in each sentence below. Write the word parts in the blanks. If a word does not have a prefix or suffix, write "none" in the blank. Some of the words contain word parts you learned in earlier lessons. Give the meaning of the whole word. Then check your meaning to see if it makes sense in the context.

1. We are having *unending* computer problems due to a bad electrical circuit.

   prefix:_____   meaning: _____

   suffix:_____   meaning: _____

   root: _____   meaning: _____

   meaning of full word: _____

2. The customer was *unyielding* in her demands.

   prefix:_____   meaning: _____

   suffix:_____   meaning: _____

   root: _____   meaning: _____

   meaning of full word: _____

3. The stockholders were *unimpressed* by the report.

   prefix:_____   meaning: _____

   suffix:_____   meaning: _____

   root: _____   meaning: _____

   meaning of full word: _____

4. He *denounced* the report as meaningless.

   prefix:_____   meaning: _____

   suffix:_____   meaning: _____

   root: _____   meaning: _____

   meaning of full word: _____

5. Please do this with *expediency*.

   prefix:_____   meaning: _____

   suffix:_____   meaning: _____

   root: _____   meaning: _____

   meaning of full word: _____

Answers to Skills Practice Exercise are on page 148.

Check Yourself

Work Problem

The Coverall Insurance Company has decided to use its own staff to handle all repairs to buildings and equipment. The company has expanded the repair and maintenance department to do this. Maintenance supervisor Jim Greene drew a flowchart showing the work flow in his department. Each department will be billed for the work it requests. Mr. Greene asks you to learn the chart so you can help your coworkers learn the new system.

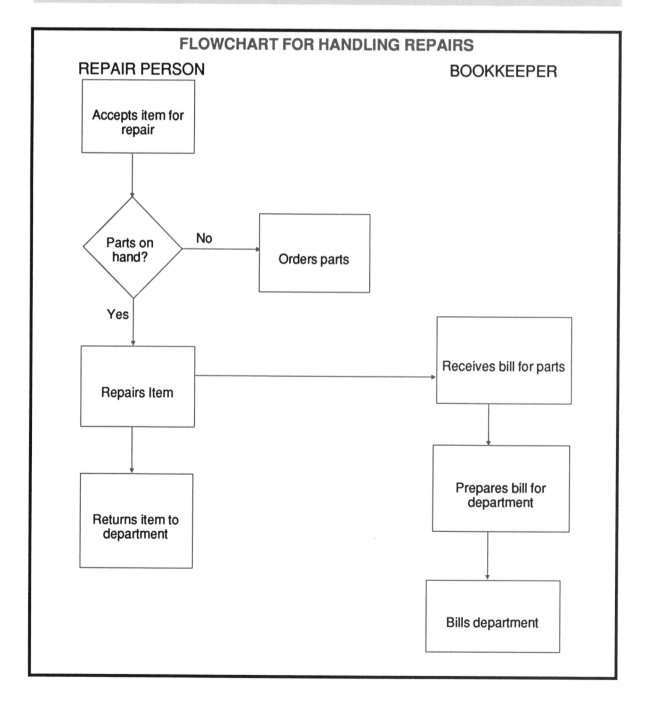

Exercise

As you read, try to find the meaning of any difficult words you find. Consider the words with prefixes or suffixes listed below. Write the word parts and their meanings in the blanks. Then give the meaning of the whole word. You may use a dictionary to check your work.

1. submits

   prefix:_____   meaning: _____

   suffix:_____   meaning: _____

   root: _____   meaning: _____

   meaning of full word: _____

2. transmits

   prefix:_____   meaning: _____

   suffix:_____   meaning: _____

   root: _____   meaning: _____

   meaning of full word: _____

3. computes

   prefix:_____   meaning: _____

   suffix:_____   meaning: _____

   root: _____   meaning: _____

   meaning of full word: _____

4. verify

   prefix:_____   meaning: _____

   suffix:_____   meaning: _____

   root: _____   meaning: _____

   meaning of full word: _____

5. available

   prefix:_____   meaning: _____

   suffix:_____   meaning: _____

   root: _____   meaning: _____

   meaning of full word: _____

Now consider your work problem and the chart you are reading. Answer the following questions. Remember to define, plan, read, and check.

What is your purpose for reading this chart?

_____

_____

What will the repair people do if they do not have the needed parts?

_____

_____

What do the repair people do after an item has been repaired?

_____

_____

What do the bookkeepers do after they receive the bill for the parts?

_____

_____

Answers to Problem-Solving Practice Questions

Define Your Problem

What is my purpose for reading this material?

To discover whether I should call copier repair service.

What should I be able to do when I finish reading?

Know whether copy machine must be fixed by professional.

Plan Your Solution

What information do I need from this material to solve my work problem?

Whether copy machine problem is one I can fix myself.

How carefully will I have to read to find the information I need?

Follow steps of flowchart, answer questions, and move according to arrows.

Read

What information do the format clues give me?

Begin at top and follow arrows.

What do I already know about this situation that will help me?

I've run the copier and am familiar with it.

Should I continue reading this material?

Yes, until I have answer about calling service rep.

What information is important because it helps me solve my work problem?

Each block is important because it helps me reach a decision.

Did I organize the information to carry out the directions?

Yes.

| Check Your Solution |

Did I accomplish my purpose? (Was I able to carry out the directions?)

Yes. I will decide whether to call repair service.

Did the information help me solve my work problem? How?

Yes. Following the chart directions, I have made the appropriate decision.

Answers to Skills Practice Exercise

1. prefix: *un-*
   suffix: *-ing*
   root: *end*
   word meaning: "not stopping"
2. prefix: *un-*
   suffix: *-ing*
   root: *yield*
   word meaning: "not giving up"
3. prefix: *un-*
   suffix: *-ed*
   root: *impress*
   word meaning: "not influenced"
4. prefix: *de-*
   suffix: *-ed*
   root: *nounce*
   word meaning: "bad mouthed"
5. prefix: *ex-*
   suffix: *-iency*
   root: *ped*
   word meaning: "haste"

On the job, the most common reference books you will read to follow directions will be manuals. Most often these will be manuals telling how to operate equipment. Large companies might also have policy or procedural manuals. These manuals give directions for carrying out tasks or discuss how employees should handle certain work situations. For example, a procedural manual might tell employees what to do in case of a fire.

Reading to Follow Directions

Accounting manager Robert Gaines has a new computer program. He must install it on his computer. Look at how he uses the reading steps to read a page in the manual to follow instructions.

1. He looks for information from the format clues. (The heading tells him about the directions on this page.)

4. He identifies the information that is important because it helps him solve his work problem. (Most of the information is important. The paragraphs at the bottom starting with *if* may be less important than the others.)

5. He organizes the information to carry out the directions. (He decides to use the checklist top to bottom to be sure he takes all the steps.)

How To Use This Manual

• Make sure your program package is complete by using the checklist in Chapter 1.

• Make sure your computer's memory is configured (set to work) correctly. Read the section in Chapter 2 that applies to your operating system for information on memory needs.

• Make sure you make all needed changes to your operating system files.

• Use the Install program to transfer the 1-2-3 Release 3 program files to your hard disk and choose the equipment you will use with 1-2-3.

• Start 1-2-3 and change your default directory if you have a separate directory for your data files.

• If you change the equipment you use with 1-2-3, you will need to use the Install program again. Read Chapter 4 to change the equipment selections you made the first time you installed 1-2-3.

• If you change the operating system you use with 1-2-3, you will need to use the Install program again. Read the section in Chapter 2 that applies to your operating system and then read Chapter 4 to change your operating system selection.

2. He looks for what he already knows about this situation that will help him. (He already knows a lot about his computer and has installed programs on it before. Some of what he reads he will already know.)

3. He decides whether to continue reading this material. (Yes, to be sure he understands and carries out all the directions.)

You have seen how Robert Gaines read to follow directions in a manual. Before reading, he used the problem-solving strategy. Let's go through another work problem using this problem-solving strategy.

Work Problem

Computer training coordinator Alison Leonard has just received the new company procedures manual. She sees a new section on telephone procedures. Ms. Leonard often uses the telephone in her job. Below is a page from the manual:

Coverall Insurance Company Procedures Manual   page 9

TELEPHONE CALL PROCEDURES

Much of our business is done over the phone. A telephone call is often the first contact a person has with us. For many of our customers, the only contact they have with our firm is over the phone. Many of our employees make and receive several calls a day. Our success depends on how well we use our telephones. These procedures are to make sure that everyone who has telephone contact with us has a pleasant experience.

Procedures for All Calls

- Use the person's last name and title, unless it is an acquaintance or the person suggests you use first names.

- Have person's name written down correctly in front of you. If you do not know it, ask for the spelling.

- End calls gracefully. If you are the caller, say "Thank you," wait for response, then hang up. If you got the call, let the caller end the call.

Procedures for Incoming Calls

- Answer calls promptly.

- Identify yourself, position, and company immediately.

- Always ask permission before putting anyone on hold.

- Always use the approved telephone message forms to make sure you take complete, accurate messages.

Define Your Problem

What is my purpose for reading this material?

To find out company telephone procedures.

What should I be able to do when I finish reading?

Follow company procedures to handle telephone calls.

Plan Your Solution

What information do I need from this material to solve my work problem?

Specific steps to follow when making and receiving telephone calls.

How carefully will I have to read to find the information I need?

Carefully because I make and receive many telephone calls.

Read

What information do the format clues give me?

Procedures manual. Page heading tells me page is about phone calls. Other headings on kinds of calls.

What do I already know about this situation that will help me?

I already know a lot about using telephone, so instructions easy to understand.

Should I continue reading this material?

Yes. I need to know what to do.

What information is important because it helps me solve my work problem?

The specific procedures for all calls and those for incoming calls.

Did I organize the information to carry out the directions?

Yes.

Check Your Solution

Did I accomplish my purpose? (Was I able to carry out the directions?)

Yes. I know the company procedures for telephone calls.

Did the information help me solve my work problem? How?

Yes. I can follow the directions to make and receive calls correctly.

Problem-Solving Practice

Now apply your strategy to another work problem.

Work Problem

You are working as an assistant to Jim Greene. He is supervisor of the maintenance department. He has prepared a department manual with instructions for handling emergencies or equipment failures.

He wants you to know these directions. He says, "Be sure you know what to do if the heat goes off. The company has a lot of computers. A sudden change in the temperature could hurt them." You look in the department manual for what to do if the oil burner fails.

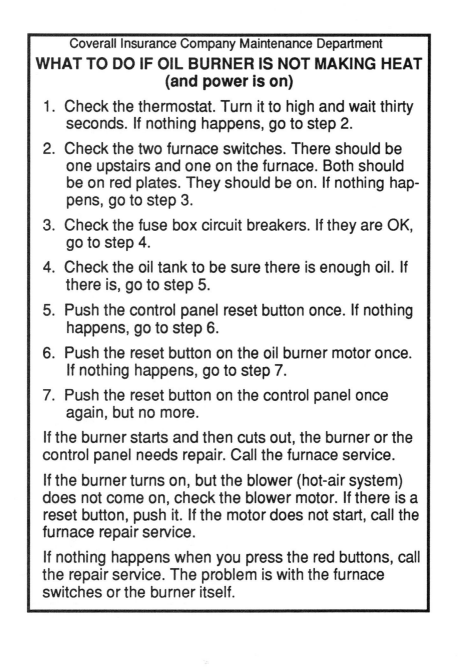

Coverall Insurance Company Maintenance Department

WHAT TO DO IF OIL BURNER IS NOT MAKING HEAT (and power is on)

1. Check the thermostat. Turn it to high and wait thirty seconds. If nothing happens, go to step 2.

2. Check the two furnace switches. There should be one upstairs and one on the furnace. Both should be on red plates. They should be on. If nothing happens, go to step 3.

3. Check the fuse box circuit breakers. If they are OK, go to step 4.

4. Check the oil tank to be sure there is enough oil. If there is, go to step 5.

5. Push the control panel reset button once. If nothing happens, go to step 6.

6. Push the reset button on the oil burner motor once. If nothing happens, go to step 7.

7. Push the reset button on the control panel once again, but no more.

If the burner starts and then cuts out, the burner or the control panel needs repair. Call the furnace service.

If the burner turns on, but the blower (hot-air system) does not come on, check the blower motor. If there is a reset button, push it. If the motor does not start, call the furnace repair service.

If nothing happens when you press the red buttons, call the repair service. The problem is with the furnace switches or the burner itself.

Define Your Problem

What is my purpose for reading this material?

_____

_____

What should I be able to do when I finish reading?

_____

_____

Plan Your Solution

What information do I need from this material to solve my work problem?

_____

_____

_____

_____

How carefully will I have to read to find the information I need?

_____

_____

_____

Read

What information do the format clues give me?

_____

_____

_____

_____

What do I already know about this situation that will help me?

_____

_____

_____

Should I continue reading this material?   _____

_____

What information is important because
it helps me solve my work problem?   _____

_____

_____

_____

Did I organize the information to carry
out the directions?   _____

_____

_____

| Check Your Solution |

Did I accomplish my purpose? (Was I
able to carry out the directions?)   _____

_____

_____

_____

Did the information help me solve my
work problem? How?   _____

_____

_____

_____

Answers to the Problem-Solving Practice questions are on pages 163-164.

On Your Own

Now you will read more manual pages to follow directions. Remember to define your purpose and plan your solution. Read and, if you need to, reread the pages carefully. Finally, check to see if you have solved your problem.

Work Problem A

Sales manager Alice Roman must work with customers in Ireland. Ms. Roman often asks you to place international calls for her. Direct dialing saves the company money, and dialing mistakes waste time. Ms. Roman tells you to read the directions in the front of the telephone book for making international calls.

INTERNATIONAL CALLING—How to Make International Calls

You can dial many international calls directly unless the first three digits of your telephone number are: 393, 420, 521, 561, 568, 569, 774, 779.

Dialing Direct Costs Less.

To place an international call, dial:
011 (International access code)
  + the two- or three-digit country code
  + the one- to five-digit city code
  + the local number

If you are calling from a Touch-Tone telephone, press the # button after dialing the entire number. This will speed your call along.

For example:
To place a call to Frankfurt, Germany, dial:
011   (International Access Code)
  49   (Country Code)
  69   (City code)
        (Local Number)

*The time column is used to calculate the time in the country you are calling. Add the hours opposite your country to Eastern Standard time.

Country Codes		City Codes (Major Cities)	Time
IRELAND	353	Cork 21, Dublin 1, Galway 91, Limerick 61, Waterford 51	5
UNITED KINDOM	44	Belfast 232, Birmingham 21, Cardiff 222, Edinburgh 31, Glasgow 41, Leeds 532, London 1, Manchester 61	5

What is your purpose for reading this page?

_____

_____

What three digits must you dial first to call another country? What are these numbers called?

_____

_____

What numbers do you dial to reach Dublin? To reach Galway?

_____

_____

What button do you press to speed your call along?

_____

_____

Work Problem B

Alice Roman wants to be sure that all letters that leave the Coverall office are accurate, well written, and correct. She gives you the company procedures manual. It includes a section on checking letters before they are sent. She tells you to follow its directions to check each letter before you send it.

Coverall Insurance Company Procedures Manual   page 22

PROCEDURE FOR CHECKING LETTERS

1. Read through the letter once for sense.
2. Read it again for style, consistency, and grammar.
3. Check names and addresses with great care.
4. Check numbers, especially decimals.
5. Double-check all totals.
6. Check all lists to make sure numbers are in correct order.
7. Use a dictionary or reference book if uncertain.

What is your purpose for reading this page?

_____

_____

What is the first thing you should check? Why?

_____

_____

Why read the letter again?

_____

_____

What should you do when you are not sure if something is correct?

_____

_____

Work Problem C

Alice Roman uses a fax machine to speed up ordering supplies. She gives you the manual for the machine and asks you to read the directions for using the fax. You use the table of contents to find the instructions and then you read them.

FAX OPERATING INSTRUCTIONS

Inserting a Message

To insert a message into the fax's feeder:

1. Adjust the feeder guides to your message's width.

2. Insert your message face down into the feeder. Your fax will hold up to fifteen sheets. You can add more pages to your feeder during transmission. The feeder will advance the bottom pages into the fax.

3. Press Mode/Select to set the resolution (sharpness). *Normal* is good for most typed messages. *Fine* is good for detailed or handwritten messages. *Super-fine* reproduces the detail of complicated drawings.

4. Press Original/Cancel to select the contrast setting needed. *Normal* is good for most messages. *Dark* lightens dark messages. *Light* darkens weak, washed-out images.

5. Begin transmission.

Messages that cannot be transmitted:
Extremely thin or wrinkled pages
Pages with staples, glue, tape or paper clips
Pages with duplicating carbon on one side
Newspaper

What is your purpose for reading these instructions?

_____

_____

What adjustments can you make when you insert a message to be faxed?

_____

_____

How do you insert the page? How many sheets can you insert at once?

_____

_____

What do you press to set the resolution? Which setting is used for most pages?

_____

_____

What are some things you cannot send with a fax?

_____

_____

Work Problem D

Alice Roman wants you to help the busy salespeople in her department by setting up appointments for them. She hands you the department's manual and asks you to read the directions for setting up appointments by phone.

Coverall Insurance Company Procedures Manual   page 32

HOW TO MAKE APPOINTMENTS BY PHONE

1. Start by using the person's name. Say, "Hello, (person's last name and title)."

2. Identify yourself and tell the customer that you are calling for Coverall Life Insurance.

3. Ask the person if he or she has a moment to speak on the phone.

4. Describe briefly the service that the salespeople offer.

5. Explain that the salesperson would need only ten or fifteen minutes of their time.

6. Ask what time would be most convenient for an appointment.

7. Close politely by saying "Thank You, (person's name)."

What is your purpose for reading these instructions?

_____

_____

How should you begin your call?

_____

_____

What should you do after identifying yourself?

_____

_____

What must you explain to the person?

_____

_____

Skills Practice: Finding a Word's Meaning

You have already learned several prefixes, root words, and suffixes. You may have read more unfamiliar words in this lesson. For example, the computer program manual contained this sentence:

Make sure your computer's memory is *configured* correctly.

Do you know what *configured* means? Can you decide what it means by looking at its parts. First there is the prefix *con-*. As you know, this prefix means "with, together." The root *figure* means "a device or form."

Configured means "the joining together of different devices."

Exercise

Read the following sentences. Look at the word in italics in each sentence. Write the parts of the word in the blanks. If the word does not have one of the parts, write "none" in the blank. Some of the words contain parts you learned in earlier lessons. Give the meaning of the whole word. Check your meaning to see if it makes sense in the sentence.

1. Make sure you make all *modifications* to your operating system files.

   prefix:_____   meaning: _____

   suffix:_____   meaning: _____

   root: _____   meaning: _____

   meaning of full word: _____

2. Much of our business is *conducted* over the phone.

   prefix:_____   meaning: _____

   suffix:_____   meaning: _____

   root: _____   meaning: _____

   meaning of full word: _____

3. End calls *gracefully*.

   prefix:_____   meaning: _____

   suffix:_____   meaning: _____

   root: _____   meaning: _____

   meaning of full word: _____

4. Check the *thermostat*.

   prefix:_____   meaning: _____

   suffix:_____   meaning: _____

   root: _____   meaning: _____

   meaning of full word: _____

5. Push the *reset* button on the oil burner motor once.

prefix:_____   meaning: _____

suffix:_____   meaning: _____

root: _____   meaning: _____

meaning of full word: _____

Answers to Skills Practice Exercise are on page 165.

Check Yourself

Work Problem

Your supervisor, Robert Gaines, has a new accounting program called Star Accounting. He asks you to install the program into the computer. He reminds you to read the instructions in the manual.

MANUAL
Installation Checklist

1. Check the hardware and software requirements for the system. See page 2.1.

2. Make working copies of the Star Accounting distribution disks. See page 2.4.

3. Load the Star Accounting program onto your computer. See page 2.6.

4. Review the chapter *How to Enter Information Using Star Accounting*. See page 2.11.

5. Review Chapter 1 of the *Accounting Primer and Tutorial* manual.

6. Run the tutorials for the modules you are installing. See Chapters 2-9 of the *Accounting Primer and Tutorial manual*.

What is your purpose for reading this checklist?

_____

_____

What do you need to check first? What page should you read to do this?

_____

_____

What will you need to copy?

_____

_____

Where do you look for information on how to install the program?

_____

_____

What does the final step ask you to do?

_____

_____

Exercise

Look at the words below. Identify the prefix, root, and suffix of each. If the words do not have a prefix or suffix, write "none." Then write a sentence using the word.

1. reunite

    prefix:_____   meaning: _____

    suffix:_____   meaning: _____

    root: _____   meaning: _____

    sentence: _____

2. deductions

    prefix:_____   meaning: _____

    suffix:_____   meaning: _____

    root: _____   meaning: _____

    sentence: _____

3. transform

    prefix:_____   meaning: _____

    suffix:_____   meaning: _____

    root: _____   meaning: _____

    sentence: _____

4. unavoidable

    prefix:_____   meaning: _____

    suffix:_____   meaning: _____

    root: _____   meaning: _____

    sentence: _____

5. automatically

    prefix:_____   meaning: _____

    suffix:_____   meaning: _____

    root: _____   meaning: _____

    sentence: _____

Answers to Problem-Solving Practice Questions

Define Your Problem

What is my purpose for reading this material?

Find out what to do if heat goes off.

What should I be able to do when I finish reading?

Follow directions or tell others what to do if heat fails.

Plan Your Solution

What information do I need from this material to solve my work problem?

Steps to take if heat fails.

How carefully will I have to read to find the information I need?

Carefully, to be sure that I know all the steps to take.

Read

What information do the format clues give me?

Title, headings tell me it is what I need.

What do I already know about this situation that will help me?

I know something about furnaces, which will help me with the directions.

Should I continue reading this material?

Yes.

What information is important because it helps me solve my work problem?

All the directions.

Did I organize the information to carry out the directions?

Yes.

Check Your Solution

Did I accomplish my purpose? (Was I able to carry out the directions?)

Yes. I know the steps to take when the heat fails.

Did the information help me solve my work problem? How?

Yes. I can do what is necessary when the heat fails.

1. prefix: none
   suffix: *-tions* makes verb a noun, change
   root: *modifi* means "to change"
   word meaning: modifications is another word for "changes"
2. prefix *con-* means "with, together"
   suffix: none
   root: *duct* means "take" or "lead"
   word meaning: conduct means "to carry out"
3. prefix: none
   suffix: *-fully* means "full of"
   root: *grace* means "charm, skill"
   word meaning: gracefully means "full of charm or skill"
4. prefix: *therm-* means "heat"
   suffix: none
   root: *stat* means "fixed"
   word meaning: thermostat means "heat level is set or fixed"
5. prefix *re-* means "do it again"
   suffix: none
   root: *set* means "a position, place"
   word meaning: *reset* means "to put it back as it was"

Putting It All Together

You are back at your summer job at MailMart. Remember that this large firm sells clothing and sporting goods throughout the country. It sells mostly through catalogs. It also runs one large store.

| Work Problem A |

Today you have the job of handling complaint calls from customers. Darcie Turner says, "Many times, the customer has given us wrong information, and that is why wrong items were sent. We must be able to explain to customers what was wrong without making them more angry."

She adds, "You can expect the customer to be angry when they call. You must be able to handle this. The company has procedures to follow. Please find them and follow them."

Look at the reading material on the following pages. Read the one with the directions you need. Then answer the following questions.

Which material did you select to read?

_____

_____

In your own words, give your reasons for reading this material.

_____

_____

What are the first two things you should do when taking a complaint call?

_____

_____

What do you tell the caller you will be doing?

_____

_____

What does the policy tell you to promise the caller?

_____

_____

| Work Problem B |

Ms. Turner wants you to prepare a flowchart showing the process for handling incoming orders. "Here's a chart that explains flowchart symbols. After you have read it carefully, you will be able to follow its directions to make a flowchart."

Look at the documents on the following pages. Pick the one with the directions you need. Read it. Then answer the following questions.

Which material did you select to read?

_____

_____

In your own words, give your reasons for reading this material.

_____

_____

How many flowchart symbols are shown in the chart?

_____

_____

What does a circle mean on a flowchart? What does a rectangle mean on a flowchart?

_____

_____

Why does a diamond have two lines running from it? What do the lines mean?

_____

_____

What is the difference between a solid arrow line and a broken arrow line?

_____

_____

DATE: March 4, 199—

FROM: Israel Rojas, General Manager

TO: All Department Managers

SUBJECT: FALL CATALOG MEETING

This is to notify all department managers of the Fall Catalog Meeting. This is an important meeting to prepare the fall catalog. All managers must attend.

The meeting will be held March 18 beginning at 8:30 a.m. in the conference room. The meeting, as usual, will last all day. Please be sure to mark your calendars.

In addition to the usual items, we will discuss the following new items and prices to be included in the fall catalog. If we all agree, these will go in the catalog.

Item	Price
Crewneck Ragg Sweaters	
Men's Regular Dyed	$29.50
Men's Regular Gray	$25.50
Women's Dyed	$29.50
Women's Gray	$25.50
Shawl Collar Ragg Sweaters	
Men's Regular Dyed	$35.00
Men's Regular Gray	$32.00
Women's Dyed	$35.00
Women's Gray	$32.00
Plaid Shirts	
Men's Regular	$21.50
Men's Tall	$23.00
Women's	$21.00
Stretch Denim Jeans	
Men's	$35.00
Women's	$35.00

Thank you and see you at the meeting.

MAILMART Purchase Order Form

ORDERED BY:

Juan Cortez
1122 High Street
Coventry, RI 02816

GIFT ORDER SHIP TO:

Marc Cortez
3302 Middle Road
East Greenwich, RI 01818

Page	Stock No.	Color	Size	How Many	Description	Amount
33	3028	Blue	15½	2	Oxford cloth shirt	46.00
33	3029	White	15½	4	Oxford cloth shirt	92.00
73	8811			1	Cycling computer	41.00

PAYMENT METHOD:

CREDIT CARD NO. _____

AMOUNT ENCLOSED _____

BILL SENDER _____

Item total	179.00
Regular shipping free	
Express shipping	$8.75
TOTAL:	187.75

Special instructions:

As you can see, this order must be sent to Marc Cortez, not to me. I want it shipped express service to arrive in time for his birthday. Thank you.

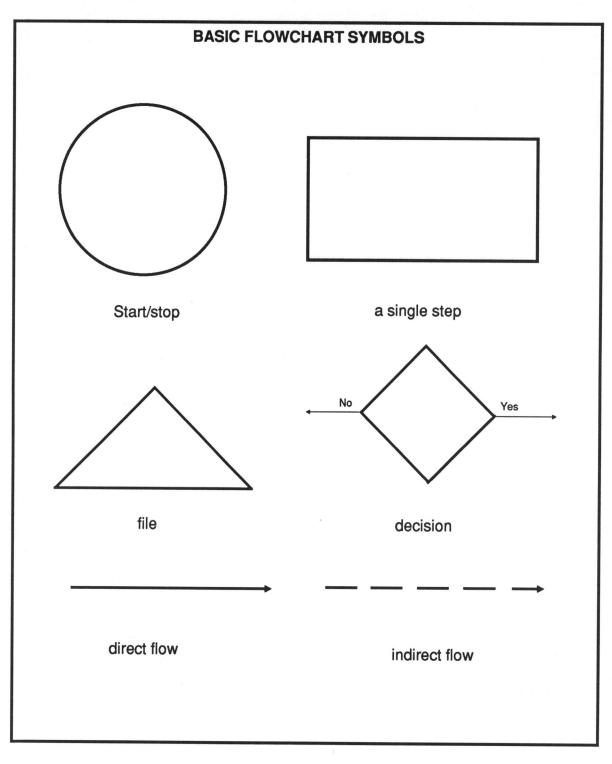

BASIC FLOWCHART SYMBOLS

Start/stop

a single step

file

decision

direct flow

indirect flow

MAILMART COMPANY POLICY MANUAL

<u>Part 3—Policies for Telephone: Handling Complaint Calls</u>

Whenever you are handling a complaint call, here is a list of what you should remember to do:

1. Slow your rate of speech.

2. Lower volume of your voice.

3. Express regret for any misunderstanding. Try to find a point of agreement.

4. Tell the caller that you will be jotting down the details as they speak to help you resolve the situation.

5. Ask intelligent questions. Listen attentively to the answers. Take accurate notes.

6. Read back what you have written. Use a lead-in phrase such as: "To make certain I understand, let's review what we've gone over . . ."

7. Tell the person making the complaint what steps you will take to correct the situation.

8. Make a promise to correct the situation THAT CAN BE KEPT.

9. Fulfill the promise.

10. Make a follow-up call to check the customer's satisfaction.

UNIT III

READING TO
CHECK INFORMATION

In Unit I, you read to find specific information. In Unit II, you followed directions. A third purpose for reading on the job is to check information. To check means to make sure the information is correct and accurate.

Using accurate information is important in business. You may need to check costs to be sure you get the best buy. You may need to check purchase order numbers, hotel reservation numbers, name spellings. The success or failure of a business rests largely on the accuracy of the information with which it works. To be sure that you are following the right directions or using the right information, you must often read to check.

When reading to check information, do the following:

1. Look for information that the format provides.

2. Look for what you already know about the situation that will help you.

3. Decide whether to continue reading the material.

4. Pick out the information that helps you solve your work problem.

5. Compare the new information with the original information.

When reading to check information, you must often read two documents and compare the new information with the original.

Corning, Rios, and Kulka

You will start Unit III working for Mari Kulka, a lawyer at the law office of Corning, Rios, and Kulka. You will have contact with some of her clients and another lawyer.

Next you will go to Major Manufacturing Company. In the personnel department, your supervisor will be Betty Santos and a coworker will be Angelo Moro. Later you will be promoted to a position in the order fulfillment department.

Next you will go to work for Don Higo at Eastern Sportscar Sales Company. Eastern Sportscar has six automobile showrooms.

You will then go to the S & G Company. You will be making travel and conference reservations for three people: Mr. Leto, Ms. Battista, and Ms. Ruis.

Once again at the end of the unit, you will return to Mailmart in the sales department, working for Darcie Turner.

LESSON 9

Reading Letters to Check Information

Companies use letters to communicate with their customers or with other companies. Information in letters is important. A company does not want to send out wrong information in a letter. Nor does a company want to take action on wrong information received. Therefore it is important to *check* information.

Like memos, business letters have a set format. Companies put their name, address, and their telephone and fax numbers at the top. This is called a letterhead.

Letterhead

> Delores Amitai
> Attorney-at-Law
> 812 Santa Anna Way
> Waco, Texas 76709
> Tel: 817-443-3381 Fax: 817-444-3241

Date it was written

> April 5, 199-

Interior address

> Ms. Mari Kulka
> Corning, Rios, & Kulka
> 67 Adams Street
> Waco, Texas 76708

Salutation, person to whom it is sent

> Dear Ms. Kulka:

Body of letter

> Last week on the phone we discussed getting together next week. I believe the date we set was Tuesday, April 12, at 10:00 at the Westover Lawyers Club.

> I am enclosing some papers on the Jones case, which you might look at before we get together.

> I look forward to meeting you and discussing the Jones case in greater detail.

Complimentary close

> Yours truly,

Signature, who it is from

> Delores Amitai

Initials of typist

> es

Copy to this person

> c: James Wong
> Encl.

Abbreviation for enclosure, indicates something enclosed with letter

Reading to Check Information

Now look at the letter again and see how Ms. Kulka reads it to check information.

1. She looks for information that the format provides. (Date, sender, something enclosed.)

2. She looks for what she already knows about this situation that will help her. (She has agreed to meet Ms. Amitai. Purpose of meeting. Enclosure relates to meeting.)

3. She decides whether to continue reading this material. (No. She will have time to read enclosed papers before meeting.)

4. She identifies the information that helps her solve her work problem. (Date, place, purpose of meeting are what she agreed to in phone conversation.)

5. She checks new information against original information. (She checks her calendar and has already written down time, place, and purpose of meeting.)

Delores Amitai
Attorney-at-Law
812 Santa Anna Way
Waco, Texas 76709
Tel: 817-443-3381 Fax: 817-444-3241

April 5, 199-

Ms. Kulka
Corning, Rios, & Kulka
67 Adams Street
Waco, Texas 76708

Dear Ms. Kulka:

Last week on the phone we discussed getting together next week. I believe the date we set was Tuesday, April 12, at 10:00 at the Westover Lawyers Club.

I am enclosing some papers on the Jones case, which you might look at before we get together.

I look forward to meeting you discussing the Jones case in greater detail.

Yours truly,

Delores Amitai

es
c: James Wong
Encl.

Ms. Kulka read to check information in a letter. She used the problem-solving strategy for reading described in the introduction. Let's go through another work problem using the problem-solving strategy.

Work Problem

Ms. Kulka is a lawyer at Corning, Rios, & Kulka, a law office. She is working on the Jones case. She leaves you a note saying she wants to meet Mr. Jones on April 26 at his office.

Mr. Jones said he would be out of town in late April. You must find out if he will be in his office on April 26. Also you must check whether his office is at 24 El Paso Boulevard. Ms. Kulka tells you to look for the information on his letter dated April 5.

```
                        William A. Jones
                      24 El Paso Boulevard
                       Waco, Texas 76708

         April 5, 199-

         Ms. Mari Kulka
         Corning, Rios, & Kulka
         67 Adams Street
         Waco, Texas 76708

         Dear Ms. Kulka:

         I am pleased to hear that you are
         making progress on my case.  My
         associate, who works closely with
         me, is Patricia Wells.  She is
         knowledgeable about the case.  You
         can call her for information if you
         cannot reach me at any time.

         I will be in Seattle from April 24
         to April 27.  I expect to get some
         information that is pertinent to
         the case.  I will share it with you
         when I return.

         Yours truly,


         William A. Jones
```

Define Your Problem

What is my purpose for reading this material?

To check info in Kulka's note against Jones' letter.

What should I be able to do when I finish reading?

Tell Ms. Kulka if she can meet April 26 with Jones. Check address.

| Plan Your Solution |

What information do I need from this material to solve my work problem?

The dates Mr. Jones will be away and the location of his office.

How carefully will I have to read to find the information I need?

Carefully enough to check two pieces of information.

| Read |

What information do the format clues give me?

From Mr. Jones to Ms. Kulka, dated April 5, 1992.

What do I already know about this situation that will help me?

The letter is the one Ms. Kulka said had the information.

Should I continue reading this material?

Not after I have checked the information.

What information is important because it helps me solve my work problem?

Location of Mr. Jones' office. Dates he will be away.

Have I checked the new information against original information?

Yes.

Check Your Solution

Did I accomplish my purpose? (Was I able to check the information?)

Yes. I checked the information.

Did the information help me solve my work problem? How?

Yes. I can tell Ms. Kulka that Mr. Jones will be away on the day she wants to meet.

Problem-Solving Practice

Now apply your reading strategy to another work problem.

Work Problem

Ms. Kulka is preparing a letter to Ms. Amitai. She asks you to look at Ms. Amitai's letter of November 30 to check the following information:

- Is Ben Miller's lawyer Jim Jackson?
- Is the court appearance on May 12?
- Is Ms. Amitai's fax number 817-444-3241?

Delores Amitai
Attorney-at-Law
812 Santa Anna Way
Waco, Texas 76709
Tel: 817-443-3381 Fax: 817-444-3241

November 30, 199-

Ms. Mari Kulka
Corning, Rios, & Kulka
67 Adams Street
Waco, Texas 76708

Dear Ms. Kulka:

We are making progress on the Ben Miller case. For your information, Mr. Miller's lawyer is Jim Jackson. I know Jim well and know he is a good attorney for this case.

We have some new evidence that will strengthen Mr. Miller's case. There are only a few problems left. The date of the court appearance is set for May 12. If we need your services again, we will let you know. Thank you for your help.

Yours truly,

Delores Amitai

Define Your Problem

What is my purpose for reading this material?

_____

_____

What should I be able to do when I finish reading?

_____

_____

Plan Your Solution

What information do I need from this material to solve my work problem?

_____

_____

_____

_____

How carefully will I have to read to find the information I need?

_____

_____

_____

Read

What information do the format clues give me?

_____

_____

_____

_____

What do I already know about this situation that will help me?

_____

_____

_____

Should I continue reading this material? _____

_____

What information is important because
it helps me solve my work problem? _____

_____

_____

_____

Have I checked the new information
against original information? _____

_____

_____

Check Your Solution

Did I accomplish my purpose? (Was I
able to check the information?) _____

_____

_____

_____

Did the information help me solve my
work problem? How? _____

_____

_____

_____

Answers to the Problem-Solving Practice questions are on pages 191-192.

On Your Own

Here are four more work problems. Remember to define your purpose and plan your solution. Read and, if you need to, reread some or all of the letters carefully. Finally, check to see if you have solved your problem.

Work Problem A

Albert Ross will be flying in from Boston. Your company made the flight arrangements. Mr. Ross calls to be sure that he has the correct information. He has Southeast Airlines, Flight No. 54. It leaves Boston at 2:30 P.M., Wednesday, June 16. You pull the travel agent's letter from the file to check the information.

```
        BUSINESS TRAVEL INC.
          232 WEST BLVD.
        WACO, TEXAS, 76708

May 30, 199-

Ms. Mari Kulka
Corning, Rios, & Kulka
67 Adams Street
Waco, Texas 76708

Dear Ms. Kulka:

We have made the following travel
arrangements for Mr. Albert Ross.
The ticket is being sent to him and
should arrive in plenty of time.

For your information, he will be on
Southeast Airlines, Flight No. 54,
Leaving Boston 1:30 p.m., Wednesday,
June 16. We were unable to get a
seat assignment for him.

Thank you for letting us serve you.

Sincerely,


Alicia Perez
Business Travel Inc.
```

What is your purpose for reading this material?

_____

_____

Does Mr. Ross have the correct information? If not, what should you tell him?

_____

_____

What might happen if Mr. Ross travels with the information he has?

_____

_____

Although he has not asked for it, what additional piece of information might you give Mr. Ross?

_____

_____

Work Problem B

The desk lamp in Ms. Kulka's office is broken. You have ordered a new one from Houston Lighting Company. Pedro Delgado from the lighting company calls to check the order. Your letter was damaged in the mail and is hard to read.

Delgado thinks you ordered model number 45-731-B, color green, and that this is a rush order. Ms. Kulka's office will pay the extra shipping charge. You pull the copy of your letter from the file to check the information.

Corning, Rios, & Kulka
67 Adams Street
Waco, Texas 76708

July 8, 199-

Mr. Pedro Delgado
Houston Lighting Company
719 Johnson Boulevard
Houston, Texas

Dear Mr. Delgado:

Our office purchased a number of
desk lamps from your company
earlier this year. Unfortunately,
one of them was broken. I would
like to order a replacement for it.
It is model number 45-731-B, and we
would like it in green. This is
not a rush, so please send the lamp
by regular mail.

Yours truly,

Your Name

What is your purpose for reading this letter?

_____

_____

Does Mr. Delgado have the correct information? If not, what is incorrect?

_____

_____

What will happen if Mr. Delgado ships the order according to the information he gives you over the phone?

_____

_____

Why was it good that Mr. Delgado called to check the information?

_____

_____

Work Problem C

Ms. Kulka is away on business. She calls you to ask if a letter has come in from Sanford Lincoln. She says, "If it has, read it. I need to know if Mr. Lincoln says his home owner's insurance covered his cameras." The following letter came today for Ms. Kulka. You open and read it. How do you respond to Ms. Kulka?

```
June 27, 199-
Ms. Mari Kulka
Corning, Rios, & Kulka
67 Adams Street,
Waco, Texas 76708

Dear Ms. Kulka:

As you suggested, I have gone
through all my papers relating to
the insurance policy.  I was sure I
had coverage for my cameras.

Two years ago I took out a policy
for them, and the premiums are paid
up.  I feel much better now about
the chances of getting my money
back from the theft. Please let me
know if you need more information.

Yours truly,


Sanford Lincoln
```

What is your purpose for reading this letter?

_____

_____

According to the letter, why did Mr. Lincoln check his insurance policy?

_____

_____

What does the letter say happened to Mr. Lincoln's cameras? Is this important information for you to know?

_____

_____

What does the letter say about insurance coverage on the cameras?

_____

_____

Work Problem D

Ms. Kulka is still away on a business trip. She calls to ask you to watch for a letter from Ms. Sally Arms. "Ms. Arms called me just before I left," Ms. Kulka tells you. "She said she might want me to help her in a dispute with her landlord. But she wasn't sure. I haven't heard anything from her since. I don't know if she still wants my help."

Ms. Kulka says to open any letter from Ms. Arms and let her know if there is any new information about her problem. The following letter arrives.

```
June 30, 199-

Ms. Mari Kulka
Corning, Rios, & Kulka
67 Adams Street,
Waco, Texas 76708

Dear Ms. Kulka:

I have called your office many
times and have been told you are
away.  I am very angry because I
thought you were looking into my
case.

My landlord is constantly calling
and threatening to evict me.  I wish
you were available to advise me.

Please call me as soon as possible.
You can call me any time at home or
at work.  You have both numbers.
Thank you.

Sincerely,


Sally Arms
```

What is your purpose for reading this letter?

_____

_____

What conclusions can you make if you compare what Ms. Kulka told you with what the letter said?

_____

_____

Considering what Ms. Arms said in the letter, what can you recommend to Ms. Kulka?

_____

_____

Skills Practice: Finding a Word's Meaning

As you have already learned, you can often decide the meaning of a word from its context. This does not always work, however. Read the following sentence.

> The oculist drives a red car.

About all this sentence tells you is that an oculist is a person old enough to drive a car. You have to check the dictionary to find the meaning of *oculist*.

Now let's look at some sentences in which the context does help you decide the meaning of a word.

Example: In the letter from William Jones to Mari Kulka, you saw this sentence:

> My *associate*, who works closely with me, is Patricia Wells.

The word *associate* may be familiar to you. Have you ever said something like, "I don't *associate* with them"? Perhaps you belong to an *association*? In this sentence Patricia Wells works closely with Mr. Jones. She is his associate or business partner.

Example: In the same letter, you saw this sentence:

> I expect to get some information that is *pertinent* to the case.

What kind of information is *pertinent* information? Mr. Jones is going to share it with his lawyer. He wants her to have information that will help settle his case. He will not give her information that has nothing to do with the case. The context tells you that *pertinent* means "useful" or "related to."

Exercise

Read the following sentences. On the blank line following each, write what the word in italics means based on the context.

1. You can call her for information because she is *conversant* with the case.

_____

2. The *counselor* on the case has all the information to settle the dispute.

_____

3. The lawyer has prepared all the *judicial* papers and sent them to the court.

_____

4. The *plaintiff's* lawyer thinks she will win the case.

_____

5. The *documentation* suggests that he is guilty.

_____

Answers to Skills Practice Exercise are on page 192.

Check Yourself

Work Problem

Ms. Kulka hands you a report she has just written. She says, "Please check that I have the information correct on the Baylor case. Have I spelled Mr. and Mrs. Baylor's first names correctly? Are they Kiel and Anna? Do I have the correct date for their first meeting with the tax auditor—July 23, 1990? And the amount of back tax they are said to owe—$1,582? Look at the letter from the Baylors in the file."

```
October 5, 199-

Ms. Mari Kulka
Corning, Rios, & Kulka
67 Adams Street,
Waco, Texas 76708

Dear Ms. Kulka:

Here is the additional information
you requested.  We met with the tax
auditor a total of four times in
1990.  The first time was on April
30, and the fourth time was on
August 12.

He asked us several questions that
had nothing to do with our
business.  We did not think he had
analyzed our tax records carefully.
We keep very good records, but he
did not know what we had paid.

He says that we owe $1,582 in back
taxes.  This is an absurd figure.
We have never owed this much in our
lives.  He must be making a
mistake.  Please let us know what
we should do next.  Thank you.

Yours truly,


Mr. Kiel Baylor
Mrs. Anna Baylor
```

Exercise

As you read, try to determine the meaning of any difficult words you find from the context. In the exercise below, circle the letter before the word that most closely matches the numbered word.

1. additional

   a) added or more
   b) inspirational
   c) taken away
   d) altogether

2. auditor

   a) a person who makes tapes
   b) an accountant
   c) a disk jockey
   d) a TV repair person

3. to analyze

   a) to request
   b) to study
   c) to call on the telephone
   d) to lose

4. absurd

   a) very good
   b) very high
   c) greenish-gray
   d) foolish, unreasonable

Now consider your work problem and the letter you are reading. Answer the following questions. Remember to define, plan, read, and check.

What is your purpose for reading this letter?

_____

_____

What was the date that the Baylors first met with the tax auditor? Is it the date that Ms. Kulka thinks it is?

_____

_____

What are Mr. and Mrs. Baylor's first names? Does Ms. Kulka have them correct?

_____

_____

What is the amount the Baylors are said to owe? Does Ms. Kulka have it correct?

_____

_____

Answers to Problem-Solving Practice Questions

Define Your Problem

What is my purpose for reading this material?

To check three pieces of information.

What should I be able to do when I finish reading?

Tell Ms. Kulka her info is correct or incorrect.

Plan Your Solution

What information do I need from this material to solve my work problem?

Name of Ben Miller's lawyer. Court appearance date. Fax number of Ms. Amitai's office.

How carefully will I have to read to find the information I need?

Carefully, to check name, fax number, and date.

Read

What information do the format clues give me?

From Ms. Amitai to Ms. Kulka.

What do I already know about this situation that will help me?

It is a letter with the right date.

Should I continue reading this material?

Yes. Confirm fax number. Confirm spelling of lawyer's name and date of court appearance.

What information is important because it helps me solve my work problem?

Fax number 817-444-3241. Date of court appearance 5/12. Lawyer's name Jim Jackson.

Have I checked the new information against original information?

Yes.

Check Your Solution

Did I accomplish my purpose? (Was I able to check the information?)

Yes. I can confirm all the information Ms. Kulka gave me.

Did the information help me solve my work problem? How?

Yes. I have solved my problem because I have been able to check all the information.

Answers to Skills Practice Exercise

1. *conversant* means "knowledgeable, knows about"
2. *counselor* means "lawyer, attorney"
3. *judicial* means "legal"
4. *plaintiff* means "person making the complaint, bringing the court suit"
5. *documentation* means "papers, documents"

LESSON 10

Reading Forms to Check Information

You read several different forms in earlier lessons. Now you will look at forms again, this time to check information. Forms often use a lot of numbers. When checking numbers, you have to read carefully. It is easy to read numbers incorrectly.

Here is an invoice sent to Angelo Moro in the personnel department of the Major Manufacturing Company.

Whom invoice is from →	**Elton Office Electronics**	23 Fairview Avenue St. Paul, MN 55116
	INVOICE: 2435	Tel: 612-005-2112 Fax: 612-522-1001

Whom invoice is to →

How item to be shipped →

Account #: Maj744	Date: 10/15/199-
Bill to: Major Manufacturing Co. 181 Gorham Road Alton, Il 62002	Attn: Angelo Moro

Purchase order number ←

Ship Rush __ Normal _X_	Purchase Order No. 68-2934-77

Item number →

What item is →

Item No.	Description	Quantity	Unit Price	Cost
CA-872	Desktop Calculator with Printer	5	30.00	$150.00

Price of one item →

How many of the item shipped →

	Subtotal:	$150.00 ←
	Shipping:	
	Sales Tax:	9.00 ←
	Total Due:	$159.00 ←

Price for all items

Sales tax on all 5 items

Please return pink copy with payment.

Amount to be paid by Major

193

Reading to Check Information

Now look at the invoice again and see how Angelo reads it to check information.

1. He looks for information from the format clues. (It is from Elton Office Electronics.)

2. He looks for what he already knows about this situation that will help him. (It is an invoice for five desktop calculators with printers.)

4. He identifies the information that helps him solve his work problem. (He looks for the purchase order number.)

3. He decides whether to continue reading this material. (Yes, to be sure the price is what he expected.)

Elton Office Electronics			23 Fairview Avenue St. Paul, MN 55116	
INVOICE: 2435			Tel: 612-005-2112 Fax: 612-522-1001	

Account #: Maj744	Date: 10/15/199–
Bill to: Major Manufacturing Co. 181 Gorham Road Alton, Il 62002	Attn: Angelo Moro

Ship Rush __ Normal _X_			Purchase Order No. 68-2934-77	
Item No.	Description	Quantity	Unit Price	Cost
CA-872	Desktop Calculator with Printer	5	30.00	$150.00
			Subtotal:	$150.00
			Shipping:	
			Sales Tax:	9.00
			Total Due:	$159.00

Please return pink copy with payment.

5. He checks new information with the original. (He checks the purchase order number and item numbers on the purchase order to see if they are the same on the invoice. He checks the price on the invoice to see if it is what he expected.)

Angelo read to check information on a form. Before reading, he used the problem-solving strategy for reading. Let's go through another work problem using the problem-solving strategy.

Work Problem

You work with Angelo in the personnel department at Major. You have a memo from the president dated Sept. 25. It says a new company logo has been designed. From now on, you should use only stationery and envelopes with the new logo.

This morning a carton from Rutledge Stationery arrives in your office. On the outside is a flap that says "packing slip enclosed." You pull out the packing slip to see what is in the carton.

PACKING SLIP

Rutledge Stationery
2323 West Road, St. Paul, MN 55116

Date Shipped: 9/20/9-   No: TWG-10573

Ship To:

```
Major Manufacturing Company
181 Gorham Road
Alton, IL 62002
```

Quantity: 2500

Description: #10 Envelopes

Weight: 20 lbs
No. of Pkg. in Shipment: 3

Define Your Problem

What is my purpose for reading this material?

To check whether envelopes have old or new logo.

What should I be able to do when I finish reading?

Keep or discard envelopes.

Plan Your Solution

What information do I need from this material to solve my work problem?

Were envelopes ordered before memo from president came out?

How carefully will I have to read to find the information I need?

Skim for the date on the packing slip.

Read

What information do the format clues give me?

Headings help me find information easily.

What do I already know about this situation that will help me?

A packing slip tells me what is in the package and when it was shipped.

Should I continue reading this material?

No.

What information is important because it helps me solve my work problem?

Shipping date on packing slip.

Have I checked the new information against original information?

Yes.

Check Your Solution

Did I accomplish my purpose? (Was I able to check the information?)

Yes. Envelopes probably have old logo.

Did the information help me solve my work problem? How?

Yes. I can probably get rid of the envelopes, but I'll check them first.

Problem-Solving Practice

Now apply your reading strategy to another work problem.

Work Problem

Your supervisor, Betty Santos, hands you a check prepared by the accounting department. She wants you to mail it. "But first," she says, "check and record exactly what the check is for."

You know Major recently hired two engineers, who were sent by the Daniels Employment Agency. You look for a bill from the agency and see the fee for hiring Jonathan Miller is $1245. You have not received a bill for Ralph Andrews. You check the information you have with the information you read on the check.

Major Manufacturing Company   182739
181 Gorham Road
Alton, IL 62002   *Sept. 24* 19 *9-*

Pay to the Order of: *Daniels Employment Agency* $ *1245.00*

One Thousand Two Hundred Forty-five   Dollars

Alton Bank of Commerce   *P. J. Larkin*
Alton, Illinois 62002

Define Your Problem

What is my purpose for reading this material?

_____

_____

What should I be able to do when I finish reading?

_____

_____

_____

_____

Plan Your Solution

What information do I need from this
material to solve my work problem?

_____

_____

_____

_____

How carefully will I have to read to find
the information I need?

_____

_____

_____

Read

What information do the format clues
give me?

_____

_____

_____

_____

What do I already know about this
situation that will help me?

_____

_____

_____

Should I continue reading this material?

_____

_____

_____

_____

What information is important because
it helps me solve my work problem?

_____

_____

_____

_____

Have I checked the new information
against original information?

_____

_____

_____

| Check Your Solution |

Did I accomplish my purpose? (Was I
able to check the information?)

_____

_____

_____

_____

Did the information help me solve my
work problem? How?

_____

_____

_____

_____

Answers to the Problem-Solving Practice questions are on pages 211-213.

On Your Own

Here are four more work problems. Remember to define your purpose and plan your solution. Read to check information. Then, if you need to, reread some or all of the forms carefully. Finally, check to see if you have solved your problem.

Work Problem A

You have just received a shipment from Rutledge Stationery. It contains 500 expense report forms and twenty reams of stationery. The invoice is enclosed. There is another item listed on the invoice.

You check the invoice with the purchase order in your file. Usually you give all invoices to your boss to approve for payment. Is this invoice ready for her to approve? Here are the invoice and the purchase order.

Rutledge Stationery		2323 West Road St. Paul, MN 55116		
INVOICE: 8724		Tel: 612-550-1112 Fax: 612-550-2221		
Ship to:	Major Manufacturing Co. 181 Gorham Road Alton, IL 62002	**Attn:** Mary O'Neil		
Bill to:	Major Manufacturing Co. 181 Gorham Road Alton, IL 62002	**Attn:** Mary O'Neil		
	Date Shipped: 11/22/9–	Ship Via: Truck	Purchase Order No. 21-0843	
Item No.	Description	Quantity	Unit Price	Cost
FB529	Calendars	75	2.75	$206.25
ST110	ExpnRpt	500		250.00
ST276	Stnry	20	7.50	150.00
			Subtotal:	$606.25
			Shipping:	15.00
			Sales Tax:	45.00
			Total Due:	$666.25
Please enclose yellow copy with payment.				

```
┌─────────────────────────────────────────────────────────────┐
│ Major Manufacturing                                           │
│ 181 Gorham Road          P.O. No. 21-0843                     │
│ Alton, IL 62002                       _____             │
│                                                               │
│ Tel: 618-333-3333  Fax: 618-222-2222  PURCHASE ORDER          │
│  ╭──────────────────────────────────────────────────────╮    │
│  │ VENDOR:                                                │    │
│  │ Rutledge Stationery                                    │    │
│  │ 2323 West Road                                         │    │
│  │ St. Paul, MN 55116                                     │    │
│  ╰──────────────────────────────────────────────────────╯    │
│ ┌──────────────────────┬──────────────────────────────────┐  │
│ │ Date: 10/29/9-       │ Date Required:                    │  │
│ ├──────────┬───────────┼─────────────┬───────────┬────────┤  │
│ │ QUANTITY │ ITEM NO.  │ DESCRIPTION │ UNIT PRICE│ PRICE  │  │
│ ├──────────┼───────────┼─────────────┼───────────┼────────┤  │
│ │   75     │ FB529     │ Calendars   │  $2.75    │$206.25 │  │
│ │  500     │ ST110     │ Expn Rpts   │           │$250.00 │  │
│ │   20     │ ST276     │ Stnry       │  $7.50    │$150.00 │  │
│ │          │           │             │           │        │  │
│ └──────────┴───────────┴─────────────┴───────────┴────────┘  │
│ Special Instructions:                                         │
│                                                               │
│   Ship via normal ground service attn: M.                    │
│   O'Neil.                                                      │
│                                                               │
└─────────────────────────────────────────────────────────────┘
```

What is your purpose for reading these forms?

_____

_____

Check the number of items on the purchase order with the number of items on the invoice. If the number is different, explain how.

_____

_____

Check the order against the shipment. Is there a problem? If so, describe it.

_____

_____

Can your boss pay the invoice? Why?

_____

_____

Work Problem B

A week ago, you prepared two Request for Payment forms. You requested $134.65 to pay back the personnel director for travel expenses. You also requested $143.65 to pay back the assistant personnel director for travel expenses.

You receive two checks today. Read the two checks. Check them against the Request for Payment forms. Decide what to do with them.

Request For Payment

Date: 9/9/9-

For:

   Lewis A. Randall, Jr.
   Personnel Director

Amount: $134.65

Explanation: For travel expenses, as per expense report.

Request For Payment

Date: 9/9/9-

For:

   Sarah B. London
   Assistant Personnel Director

Amount: $143.65

Explanation: For travel expenses, as per expense report.

Major Manufacturing Company   182740
181 Gorham Road
Alton, IL 62002
_____ Sept. 9 _199-_

Pay to the Order of: _Lewis A. Randall, Jr._ _$134.65_

One Hundred Thirty - four and $^{65}/_{100}$ Dollars

Alton Bank of Commerce   _P. J. Larkin_
Alton, Illinois 62002

Major Manufacturing Company   182741
181 Gorham Road
Alton, IL 62002
_____ Sept. 9 _199-_

Pay to the Order of: _Sarah B. London_ _$143.65_

One Hundred Forty - three and $^{65}/_{100}$ — Dollars

Alton Bank of Commerce   _P. J. Larkin_
Alton, Illinois 62002

What is your purpose for reading these two checks?

_____

_____

How much money was requested for Lewis Randall? What is the amount on the check made out to him? Are they the same?

_____

_____

How much money was requested for Sarah London? What is the amount on the check made out to her? Are they the same?

_____

_____

Are the names of both people spelled correctly on the checks? Check them with the Request for Payment forms. Describe any differences you see.

_____

_____

Work Problem C

Ms. O'Neil shipped a package to Home Oil Company in South Bend, Indiana. It should have arrived by now. The manager at Home Oil Company called to complain that it has not.

Ms. O'Neil says, "This is the correct address and phone for Home Oil Company— 178 Hartford Avenue, South Bend, IN 46600, phone—219-778-8888." She adds, "Call Speedy Express Mail Service if there is a problem." You pull the mailing label from the file and check it with the information Ms. O'Neil gave you.

Sender's Copy   For information call 1-800-888-0000
SPEEDY EXPRESS

Sender's account #: 384756-8   Package Number: 883377000-2

Sender's address:

```
Mary O'Neil
Major Manufacturing Company
181 Gorham Road
Alton, IL 62002
```

Recipient's phone and address:

```
219-777-8888
Home Oil Company
718 Hartford Avenue
South Bend, IN 46600
```

Delivery (check one): Next AM __x__   Next PM ____   2-day ____

Package (check one): Letter: ____   Box: __x__

Payment: Bill (check one):   Sender __x__   Recipient __   Credit card ____

What is your purpose for reading this memo?

_____

_____

Check the information on this mailing label against the information Ms. O'Neil gave you. What seems to be the problem?

_____

_____

What phone number should you use to call Home Oil Company?

_____

_____

You have to call Speedy Express Company. What will you tell them?

_____

_____

Work Problem D

You have been promoted to a position in the department that fills orders. You have just received a phone call from the bookkeeper at the STG Company. He complains that they were billed for more butterfly valves than the 500 they ordered and received. The total bill is $2730.

He wants you to look into the matter. You pull the copies of the STG purchase order and the Major invoice from the file and check them. What seems to be the problem?

STG Company
1254 West Street
Chicago, IL 60600

P.O. No. 342-80843

PURCHASE ORDER

VENDOR:
Major Manufacturing Co.
181 Gorham Road
Alton, IL 62002

Date: 11/2/9–   Date Required:

QUANTITY	MODEL #	DESCRIPTION	UNIT PRICE	PRICE
500	FSB259	Butterfly valves	$5.00	$2500.00

Special Instructions:

Ship via normal routing attn: Bill Frame.

Major Manufacturing INVOICE: 8724	181 Gorham Road Alton, IL 62002 Tel: 618-333-3333 Fax: 618-222-2222

Ship to:	STG Company 1254 West Street Chicago, IL 60600	**Attn:** Bill Frame

Bill to:	STG Company 1254 West Street Chicago, IL 60600	

	Date Shipped: 11/10/9-	Ship Via: Normal	Purchase Order No. 342-80843	
Model #	**Description**	**Quantity**	**Unit Price**	**Cost**
FSB259	Butterfly valves	500	5.00	$2500.00
			Subtotal:	$2500.00
			Shipping:	25.00
			Sales Tax:	205.00
			Total Due:	$2730.00

Please enclose pink copy with payment.

What is your purpose for reading these forms?

_____

_____

How many valves were requested on the STG purchase order? How many valves were billed for on the Major invoice? Are the numbers the same?

_____

_____

Suppose you have several purchase orders from STG in your file? How do you know that this purchase order goes with this invoice?

_____

_____

Has Major correctly filled the order from STG? Why is there a difference in the amount charged?

_____

_____

Skills Practice: Finding a Word's Meaning

It is difficult to use context to find word meaning in forms because there are few sentences or paragraphs. However, if you know the general purpose of a form, you will be able to figure out what many words mean. Breaking a word into its different parts can be the most useful way to find its meaning in a form.

In the exercises below you will find some words that may be new to you. However, many of them use prefixes that you have learned earlier. Practice determining a word's meaning by looking at its separate parts.

Exercise

Read the sentences below and think about the meaning of the word in italics. Select the correct meaning for the word by circling the letter of your choice below the sentence.

1. I have added two pages to the report. Please *repaginate* the report now with the correct numbers.

    a) number the pages again
    b) read the report

2. The check must be *cosigned* before it can be cashed.

    a) signed
    b) signed by another person

3. The order cannot be shipped unless it is *prepaid*.

    a) paid before the order is shipped
    b) paid in full

4. The magazine is published *bimonthly*.

    a) every two months
    b) in two languages

5. The salespeople are *reimbursed* for their travel expenses.

    a) charged again
    b) paid back

Answers to Skills Practice Exercise are on page 213.

Check Yourself

Work Problem

Alex Chou received a check in the interoffice mail today. He gives it to you along with an invoice. He says, "This check is to pay a Rutledge invoice. Let me know which invoice it is and what item it is for. It might be for that new disk storage box. Then mail the check. Be sure to enclose the right copy of the invoice. I think they want the white one."

You take several invoices from the file and find two from Rutledge. You check them against the check to decide what to do.

Major Manufacturing Company
181 Gorham Road
Alton, IL 62002

182548

July 2 19—

Pay to the Order of: *Rutledge Stationery* $17.30

Seventeen and 30/100 ——————— Dollars

Alton Bank of Commerce
Alton, Illinois 62002

P. J. Larkin

Rutledge Stationery

INVOICE: 8341

2323 West Road
St. Paul, MN 55116

Tel: 612-550-1112
Fax: 612-550-2221

Ship to:	Major Manufacturing Co. 181 Gorham Road Alton, IL 62002		**Attn:** Alex Chou	
Bill to:	Major Manufacturing Co. 181 Gorham Road Alton, IL 62002		**Attn:** Mary O'Neil	

	Date Shipped: 6/15/9—	Ship Via: UPS	Purchase Order No. 0553-91	
Item No.	Description	Quantity	Unit Price	Cost
EQ349	electric pencil sharpener	1	$14.95	$14.95
			Subtotal:	$14.95
			Shipping:	1.60
			Sales Tax:	.75
			Total Due:	$17.30

Please enclose yellow copy with payment.

Rutledge Stationery	2323 West Road St. Paul, MN 55116
INVOICE: 9752	Tel: 612-550-1112 Fax: 612-550-2221

Ship to:	Major Manufacturing Co. 181 Gorham Road Alton, IL 62002	**Attn:** Alex Chou

Bill to:	Major Manufacturing Co. 181 Gorham Road Alton, IL 62002	**Attn:** Mary O'Neil

	Date Shipped: 6/30/9–	Ship Via: UPS	Purchase Order No. 0564-91	
Item No.	Description	Quantity	Unit Price	Cost
DB723	disk storage box	1	$17.95	$17.95

			Subtotal:	$17.95
			Shipping:	1.70
			Sales Tax:	.75
			Total Due:	$20.40

Please enclose yellow copy with payment.

Exercise

Before you complete your work problem, try to decide the meaning of the words below. Circle the letter before the word that most closely matches the numbered word.

1. recipient

   a) renter
   b) cook
   c) one who receives
   d) achieved

2. enclose

   a) wear new clothes
   b) shut
   c) put inside
   d) pull out

3. agglomerate

   a) total
   b) tremendous
   c) complete
   d) large

4. stationery

    a) bus station
    b) statue
    c) stage
    d) letterhead

5. remit

    a) offer
    b) send back payment
    c) put on gloves
    d) shown

Now consider your work problem, the invoice, and the check you are reading. Answer the following questions. Remember to define, plan, read, and check.

What is your purpose for comparing these two forms?

_____

_____

Which invoice would you say the check is for? Why?

_____

_____

Was Mr. Chou right about what the check was for?

_____

_____

What copy of the invoice do you send with the check?

_____

_____

Answers to Problem-Solving Practice Questions

Define Your Problem

What is my purpose for reading this material?

To check what the check is for.

What should I be able to do when I finish reading?

Tell supervisor what check is for.

Plan Your Solution

What information do I need from this material to solve my work problem?

Amount of check and who it is made out to.

How carefully will I have to read to find the information I need?

Skim for amount and person being paid.

Read

What information do the format clues give me?

From Major to Daniels, amount.

What do I already know about this situation that will help me?

Amount of fee and name of agency to be paid.

Should I continue reading this material?

No.

What information is important because it helps me solve my work problem?

Amount of check and name of company it is made out to.

Have I checked the new information against original information?

Yes.

Check Your Solution

Did I accomplish my purpose? (Was I able to check the information?)

Yes. Check pays Jonathan Miller's fee.

Did the information help me solve my work problem? How?

Yes. I can tell supervisor what she needs to know and send check to Daniels.

Answers to Skills Practice Exercise

1. *repaginate* means "number the pages again"
2. *cosigned* means "signed by another person"
3. *prepaid* means "paid before the order is shipped"
4. *bimonthly* means "every two months"
5. *reimbursed* means "paid back"

LESSON 11

Reading Tables and Charts to Check Information

In earlier lessons you read graphic material to find information and to follow directions. You remember that graphics are things like pie charts, bar charts, line charts, and tables. Now you will read graphic material to check information.

Here is a page from a report that Don Higo will present at the annual meeting of the Eastern Sportscar Sales Company. This year was a great year at Eastern Sportscar. Sales of the economical Jay model and the mid-priced Romeo model increased. The deluxe Stellar model remained at the same level as last year.

Don has prepared a chart to show this. Now he must check the chart with the information to check that it is correct. See the chart below that shows last year's and this year's sales.

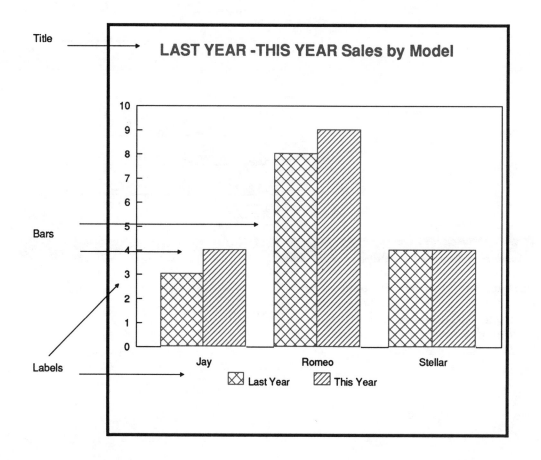

Reading to Check Information

Now look at the chart again and notice how Don Higo reads it to check information.

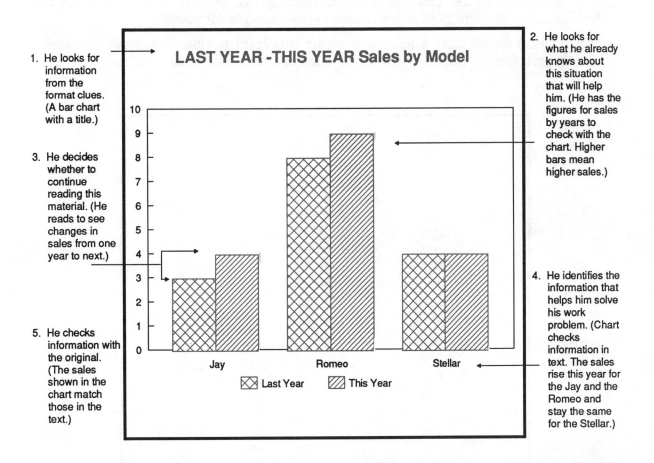

1. He looks for information from the format clues. (A bar chart with a title.)

3. He decides whether to continue reading this material. (He reads to see changes in sales from one year to next.)

5. He checks information with the original. (The sales shown in the chart match those in the text.)

2. He looks for what he already knows about this situation that will help him. (He has the figures for sales by years to check with the chart. Higher bars mean higher sales.)

4. He identifies the information that helps him solve his work problem. (Chart checks information in text. The sales rise this year for the Jay and the Romeo and stay the same for the Stellar.)

LAST YEAR - THIS YEAR Sales by Model

Last Year   This Year

Jay   Romeo   Stellar

Don Higo read to check information in a graphic. Before reading, he used the problem-solving strategy. Let's go through another work problem using the problem-solving strategy.

Work Problem

Mr. Higo wants a chart of total sales by car models. He says the sales of the Jay are one-fourth of the total sales at Eastern Sportscar. The Romeo represents half of all sales. The Stellar represents one-fourth of all sales.

He has had a pie chart prepared to show this information. You have to check the chart to see if it shows how much each car contributes to total sales.

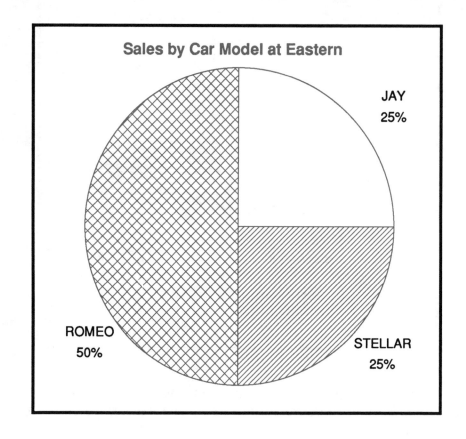

Sales by Car Model at Eastern

JAY
25%

STELLAR
25%

ROMEO
50%

Define Your Problem

What is my purpose for reading this material?

To check that it shows sales correctly.

What should I be able to do when I finish reading?

Tell Mr. Higo chart is correct or must be fixed.

Plan Your Solution

What information do I need from this material to solve my work problem?

Amount each car model sells.

How carefully will I have to read to find the information I need?

Skim for numbers. Check that numbers and chart describe similar amounts.

Read

What information do the format clues give me?

It is a pie chart that shows sales by car model.

What do I already know about this situation that will help me?

There is one slice for each car model. Size of pieces represents amount of sales.

Should I continue reading this material?

Yes, to see that each slice is right size.

What information is important because it helps me solve my work problem?

The size of the slices.

Have I checked the new information against original information?

Yes.

Check Your Solution

Did I accomplish my purpose? (Was I able to check the information?)

Yes. I found out that it showed sales correctly.

Did the information help me solve my work problem? How?

Yes. I can tell Mr. Higo that chart is correct.

Problem-Solving Practice

Now apply your strategy to another work problem.

| Work Problem |

Mr. Higo gives you a page from his report and a page with a chart on it. He says, "As I am reading this page to the group, I will show the chart on the screen. Everyone can listen to what I am saying while looking at the chart. Check the chart against the text and let me know if the chart is accurate."

Report, p. 1

Eastern Sportscar has six showrooms throughout the county. I am pleased with sales from all of them except one—the location on Route 90 in Easton.

Part of the reason for poor sales in year 10 was the repair work on the highway. No one wants to get stuck in the traffic, so they go to our other locations. Year six was an exception, and sales improved for some reason.

However, if you look at sales at Easton showroom for the past ten years, you will see that they have been declining for a long time.

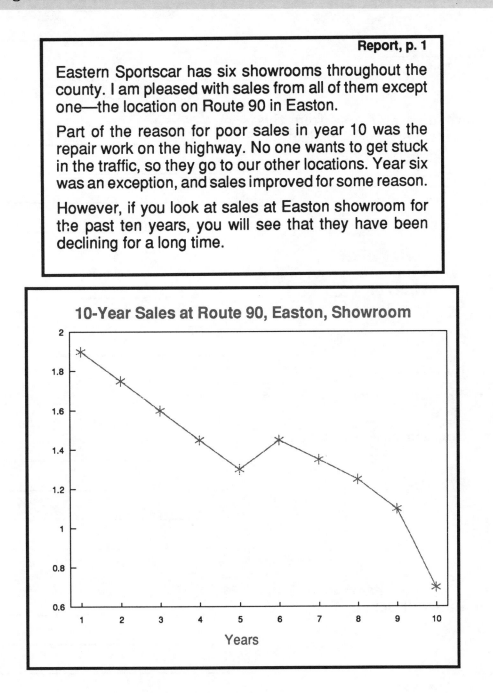

10-Year Sales at Route 90, Easton, Showroom

Define Your Problem

What is my purpose for reading this material?

_____

_____

What should I be able to do when I finish reading?

_____

_____

Plan Your Solution

What information do I need from this material to solve my work problem?

_____

_____

_____

_____

How carefully will I have to read to find the information I need?

_____

_____

_____

Read

What information do the format clues give me?

_____

_____

_____

_____

What do I already know about this situation that will help me?

_____

_____

_____

Should I continue reading this material?   _____

_____

What information is important because
it helps me solve my work problem?   _____

_____

_____

_____

Have I checked the new information
against original information?   _____

_____

_____

Check Your Solution

Did I accomplish my purpose? (Was I
able to check the information?)   _____

_____

_____

_____

Did the information help me solve my
work problem? How?   _____

_____

_____

_____

Answers to the Problem-Solving Practice questions are on pages 230-232.

On Your Own

Here are four more work problems. Remember to define your purpose and plan your solution. Read to check information. Then, if you need to, reread some or all of the information carefully. Finally, check to see if you have solved your problem.

Work Problem A

Mr. Higo has some information from the sales manager. He will use it in a monthly bulletin that will be mailed to the salesroom managers.

He gives you a page and says, "I have made a table from the information the sales manager gave me. Please check the two and let me know if the table is accurate."

```
Monthly Sales Bulletin          page 5

Here is the information on sales
for last February. I hope it helps
you. Let me know if you need more.
At the Route 90 location, we sold
14 Jays, eight Romeos, and only two
Stellars. They don't seem to be
able to move the Stellars there.

At Route 104 we sold 29 Jays, 21
Romeos and ten Stellars. And at
Ames we sold 11 Stellars—they
should do better than that—and 17
Romeos and 22 Jays.
```

SALES BY MODEL—FEBRUARY			
Location	Jay	Romeo	Stellar
Route 90	14	8	2
Route 104	29	21	10
Ames	22	17	11

What is your purpose for reading this material?

_____

_____

Check the number of Jays sold at Route 90 shown on the table and in the sales manager's report. What is the number on the table? Is the number on the table correct?

_____

_____

Check the number of Jays, Stellars, and Romeos sold at Route 104 as shown on the table and in the sales manager's report. Are the numbers on the table correct?

_____

_____

Check the rest of the numbers on the table with the numbers in the sales manager's report. Write down any that are not correct.

_____

_____

Work Problem B

Mr. Higo is the president of Eastern Sportscar. Because of the increase in sales, he has expanded and reorganized the advertising department.

- He promoted the advertising manager to director of advertising. This person now reports directly to Mr. Higo.
- He promoted two people to supervisors. These two people report to the director of advertising. One is supervisor of advertising in newspapers. The other supervisor handles radio and TV advertising.
- A second copywriter has been hired in the newspaper group. In addition, there are a designer and an assistant in this group.
- The radio and television group is smaller. There is one copywriter and an assistant in this group.

Mr. Higo has drawn a chart showing the new organization. He asks you to check to see if it is correct.

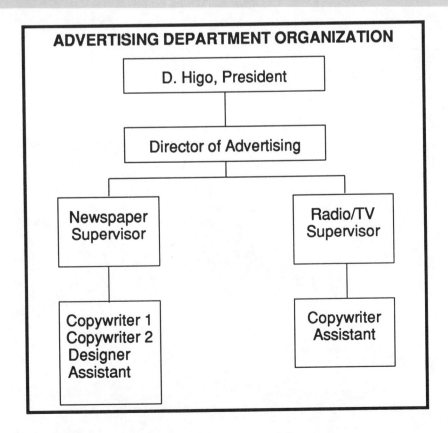

What is your purpose for reading this graphic?

_____

_____

How many people does the chart show reporting directly to Mr. Higo? Is this correct?

_____

_____

What are the titles of the supervisors? Are they shown correctly on the chart?

_____

_____

Does one group have more copywriters than the other? Is this correct?

_____

_____

Work Problem C

It is Wednesday. Mr. Higo has been at one of the other showrooms. He calls you from his car phone and asks you to check his calendar.

He says, "I am meeting Nancy Blaine from the car manufacturer for lunch. I think we said 12:30 at the Oak Tavern. I have a conference call scheduled for this afternoon at either 2:00 or 2:30. Please check my calendar for me." You look at his calendar and respond.

	Mon	**Tue**	**Wed**	**Thu**	**Fri**
08:00					
09:00	Budget Meeting 9 - 11				9:30 Conference Call
10:00					
11:00					
12:00			12:30 Oak T. N. Blaine		
01:00					
02:00	At Ames Showroom				
03:00	↓				
04:00					
05:00					

Appointment Calendar

What is your purpose for reading this graphic?

_____

_____

What information does Mr. Higo have that is correct?

_____

_____

What should you tell him about the conference call?

_____

_____

What might have happened if Mr. Higo had not called?

_____

_____

Work Problem D

You are helping Mr. Higo put together his report for the annual meeting. He hands you a chart and says, "This shows total sales estimated for next year and for five years from now. I hope I labeled everything correctly.

"Are sales of the Romeo and Stellar about the same next year? Are the Romeo sales the biggest and the Jay sales the smallest five years from now? Have I put the right title on the chart?" You look at the chart and respond.

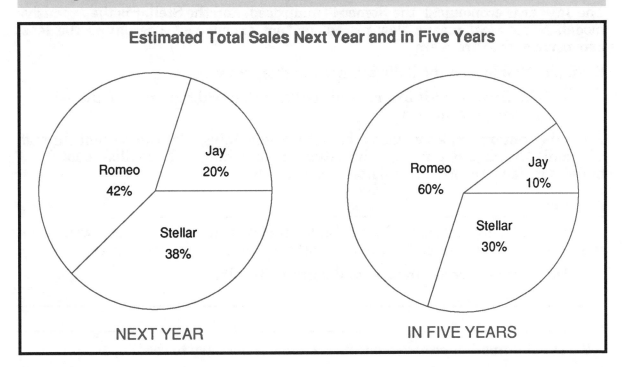

What is your purpose for reading this graphic?

_____

_____

How do you answer Mr. Higo's question about the sales of the Romeo and Stellar next year?

_____

_____

How do you answer his question about sales of the Romeo and the Jay in five years?

_____

_____

What do you tell Mr. Higo about the title of the chart? Explain your answer.

_____

_____

Skills Practice: Finding a Word's Meaning

There may have been some new words for you in this lesson. Are you getting better at deciding what they mean from context?

Example: Look at the word in italics in this sentence:

> Sales of the *economical* Jay model and the mid-priced Romeo model increased, but the expensive Stellar model sales have gone down.

The Jay car is economical, the Romeo is midpriced, and the Stellar is the expensive model. *Economical* means "low priced" or "not expensive." The Jay is the least expensive of the three cars.

Example: Now look at the italicized word in this sentence:

> He will use it in a monthly *bulletin* that will be mailed to the sales-room managers.

From the context you know that a bulletin is something that can be sent through the mail. Mr. Higo is putting information in something to be mailed monthly. A bulletin is like a report, a newsletter, or an article.

Exercise

Read the following sentences. On the blank lines following each sentence, write what the word in italics means. Then write another sentence using the word.

1. He used good *transparencies* to illustrate his talk.

   _____

   _____

2. The information *projected* on the screen was not easy to read.

   _____

   _____

3. Now that the department has been *reorganized*, Anna no longer reports to Nina.

   _____

   _____

4. We are thinking of closing the showroom because the sales there are *declining*.

   _____

   _____

5. The sales *projected* for five years from now are higher than the sales for next year.

   _____

   _____

Answers to Skills Practice Exercise are on page 232.

Check Yourself

Work Problem

You are preparing a table for Mr. Higo to use in his monthly bulletin. You must show sales for March at each of the six showrooms of Eastern Sportscar.

The showroom to be listed at the top must be the one with the highest March sales. The showroom with the next highest sales should come next and so on to the bottom. To make the table you have used information in a report from the sales manager. Check your table against the report to make any necessary corrections.

SALES MANAGER'S REPORT OF MARCH SALES

Congratulations to the Wilson showroom for making the most improvement. Wilson's sales were $300,000. Johnson's showroom had strong sales also at $280,000. Both Route 104 and Route 90 sales showed no improvement. Route 104 sales were $220,000 and Route 90 sales were $150,000.

Once again the winner was the Ames showroom at $420,000. The new showroom at Farm Center is looking pretty good. Sales there were $120,000. All in all, it was not a bad month considering the terrible weather. Let's try to do even better in April!

Eastern Sportscar Sales by Showroom in March

Location	Sales
Ames	$420,000
Wilson	$300,000
Johnson	$240,000
Route 104	$220,000
Route 90	$150,000

Exercise

Each italicized word in the sentences below starts with a prefix. Write the prefix and the word's meaning on the line below each sentence.

1. The record for the Route 90 showroom is *undistinguished*, and I cannot think of a good reason for keeping it open any longer.

   _____

2. I was able to *incorporate* the table into the report on page 12.

   _____

3. The *projector* is not plugged in so we cannot show the transparencies.

   _____

4. His voice does not *project* well, so he has to speak louder.

   _____

5. The *reorganization* plan has made a lot of people angry and upset.

   _____

Now consider your work problem. Read the table and check it against the Sales Manager's Report. Answer the following questions. Remember to define, plan, read, and check.

What is your purpose for reading this report?

_____

_____

Are all the showrooms listed? If any are not listed, write them below with their sales.

_____

_____

Check the information against the table. Are the sales shown correctly for each showroom? If any are incorrect, write them correctly below.

_____

_____

Answers to Problem-Solving Practice Questions

Define Your Problem

What is my purpose for reading this material?

To find out if information in chart is correct.

What should I be able to do when I finish reading?

Tell Mr. Nigo it is correct or what to change.

Plan Your Solution

What information do I need from this material to solve my work problem?

Route 90 sales for 10 years.

How carefully will I have to read to find the information I need?

Skim for numbers and read numbers and related information carefully.

Read

What information do the format clues give me?

Title at top. Dollars down side. Years across bottom.

What do I already know about this situation that will help me?

Sales have gone down except for one year. Chart should show this trend.

Should I continue reading this material?

Yes. I should also make sure title describes content of table.

What information is important because it helps me solve my work problem?

The line shows sales going down and matches Mr. Higo's report.

Have I checked the new information against original information?

Yes.

Check Your Solution

Did I accomplish my purpose? (Was I able to check the information?)

Yes. The information on the chart is correct.

Did the information help me solve my work problem? How?

Yes. I can tell Mr. Higo that the chart is accurate.

Answers to Skills Practice Exercise

1. *transparencies* means "words or graphics printed on clear film that can be shown on a screen"
2. *projected* means "thrown or put forward"
3. *reorganized* means "arranged or grouped differently"
4. *declining* means "going down"
5. *projected* means "expected in the future"

LESSON 12

Reading Reference
Books to Check Information

In earlier units, you read reference books to find information and to follow directions. Now you will read reference materials to check information. Some examples of reference materials are

- ✔ Directories, which list names, addresses, and phone numbers
- ✔ Buyer Guides, which list companies that sell a certain type of product
- ✔ Catalogs, which describe products sold by a company and ordering procedures
- ✔ Manuals, which contain instructions and policies

Most businesses use reference books. They use references that people have at home, such as dictionaries and phone books. They also use special types of reference books to meet their business needs. For example, in a business in which employees travel, you will find an airline directory. In a manufacturing or engineering company, you will find a dictionary of technical terms.

Here is a page from a hotel directory that Richard Leto uses when he travels to visit customers. He is planning a second trip to Maine. He wants to stay at the same hotel he stayed in the last time. He does not remember its name, but he remembers that he stayed in a large hotel with conference rooms in downtown Portland.

Information below is on hotels in Maine →

Name of the town →

Information on hotel →

Directory of United States Hotels   page 32

Hotels (Maine)

Orono
College Inn, 207-666-8000; 14 River St; 30 units, pool, sauna, restaurant on premises, rates $65-85.

Portland
Downtown Portlander Hotel, 207-775-4400; City Square South, (downtown Portland), 320 rooms, pool, 3 restaurants in hotel—others nearby, conference rooms and suites also available, rates, $100-150.
Hillsdale Inn, 207-775-1000; 87 Coastal Highway (5 miles from center of city); 25 units, pool, sauna, restaurant, rates $80-100.
Portland Hostelry, 207-775-2553; 1 Portland Square (downtown Portland), 16 units, pool, sauna, restaurant, rates $80-100.
Starlight Motel, 207-775-6000; 40 units, 46 Bay Street (in center of city), pool, restaurant, rates $70-90.

Reading to Check Information

Now look at the document again and see how Richard Leto read it to check information.

1. He looks for information from the format clues. (It lists hotels in Maine.)

2. He looks for what he already knows about this situation that will help him. (How directory and his notes are organized. Also, his experience with hotels helps him understand the information he needs.)

3. He decides whether to continue reading this material. (Yes. He wants to find the hotel in Portland where he stayed.)

4. He identifies the information that helps him solve his work problem. (He decides the hotel was the Downtown Portlander)

Directory of United States Hotels   page 32

Hotels (Maine)

Orono
College Inn, 207-666-8000; 14 River St; 30 units, pool, sauna, restaurant on premises, rates $65-85.

Portland
Downtown Portlander Hotel, 207-775-4400; City Square South, (downtown Portland), 320 rooms, pool, 3 restaurants in hotel—others nearby, conference rooms and suites also available, rates, $100-150.
Hillsdale Inn, 207-775-1000; 87 Coastal Highway (5 miles from center of city); 25 units, pool, sauna, restaurant, rates $80-100.
Portland Hostelry, 207-775-2553; 1 Portland Square (downtown Portland), 16 units, pool, sauna, restaurant, rates $80-100.
Starlight Motel, 207-775-6000; 40 units, 46 Bay Street (in center of city), pool, restaurant, rates $70-90.

---

5. He checks new information against the original. (He remembers that the hotel was large and had conference rooms.)

Richard Leto read to check information in a directory. Before reading, he used the problem-solving strategy. Let's go through another work problem using the strategy.

Work Problem

After his visit to Maine, Mr. Leto will go to Burlington, Vermont. Mr. Leto's assistant gives you his schedule and the hotel directory. He asks you to check the hotel information by comparing what is on the schedule with the information in the directory.

```
Schedule for Richard Leto, 7/18-7/20

7/18 4 P.M. Check into Radway, 18
Vermont Road, Burlington
(802-277-2000); single room (2
nights, $100 per night, charged on
Visa 132-421-306-422)

7/19 9 A.M.-1 P.M. At Burlington
office (802-277-3421)

7/19 1 P.M.-Lunch with agents at
Green Mountain Room, Radway, 18
Vermont Road, Burlington
(802-277-2005); table for 8 reserved

2-5 P.M. At Burlington office

7/20 10 A.M. Check out of Radway
```

Directory of United States Hotels   page 40

Hotels (Vermont)

Burlington

Collegetown Inn, 802-444-8000; 124 Broad St, 130 units, pool, sauna, restaurant, and coffee shop, rates $85-105, credit cards accepted: AmEx, Visa.

Burlington Hotel, 802-557-0440; Route 12 and Main, 250 units, pool, rates $95-125, credit cards accepted: AmEx, Visa

Radway Inn, 802-277-2000; 36 Mountain Highway, Route 12, 160 units, pool, Green Mountain Room Restaurant, rates $100-135, credit cards accepted: AmEx.

Define Your Problem

What is my purpose for reading this material?

To check hotel information.

What should I be able to do when I finish reading?

Tell Mr. Leto information is OK or correct it.

Plan Your Solution

What information do I need from this material to solve my work problem?

Information on Radway Inn.

How carefully will I have to read to find the information I need?

Carefully, with attention to details being checked.

Read

What information do the format clues give me?

Hotels in Vermont.

What do I already know about this situation that will help me?

Directory lists hotels in Vermont. What I already know about staying at hotels will also help.

Should I continue reading this material?

Yes, to check info on Radway in directory against schedule.

What information is important because it helps me solve my work problem?

The address. That Inn does not accept Visa credit cards.

Have I checked the new information against original information?

Yes.

| Check Your Solution |

Did I accomplish my purpose? (Was I able to check the information?)

Yes.

Did the information help me solve my work problem? How?

Yes. Phone numbers for hotels are same but addresses are different. I should call to check info.

Problem-Solving Practice

Now apply the reading strategy to another work problem.

Work Problem

Ms. Alice Battista wants you to subscribe to *Computer Trends* magazine for two years. She thinks the cost is $30 a year and that it is published in California. She warns you to order the right *Computer Trends*. A bulletin published by the Computer Society of America in Washington, D.C., is also called *Computer Trends*.

She asks you to check the information in the Publications Directory. She also wants you to find out if there are separate rates for personal and company orders.

Publications Directory   page 12

Computer Trends
88 Bay Street
Santa Cruz, CA 95060

Subscription Rates:

Personal

  One year: $20
  Two years: $37
  Five years: $80

Company

  One year: $32
  Two years: $50
  Five years: $100

Define Your Problem

What is my purpose for reading this material?

_____

_____

What should I be able to do when I finish reading?

_____

_____

Plan Your Solution

What information do I need from this
material to solve my work problem?

_____

_____

_____

_____

How carefully will I have to read to find
the information I need?

_____

_____

_____

Read

What information do the format clues
give me?

_____

_____

_____

_____

What do I already know about this
situation that will help me?

_____

_____

_____

_____

Should I continue reading this material?

_____

_____

What information is important because it helps me solve my work problem?

_____

_____

_____

_____

Have I checked the new information against original information?

_____

_____

_____

Check Your Solution

Did I accomplish my purpose? (Was I able to check the information?)

_____

_____

_____

_____

Did the information help me solve my work problem? How?

_____

_____

_____

_____

Answers to the Problem-Solving Practice questions are on pages 251-252.

On Your Own

Here are four more work problems. Remember to define your purpose and plan your solution. Read to check information. Then, if you need to, reread some or all of the reference material carefully. Finally, check to see if you have solved your problem.

Work Problem A

Richard Leto will attend a conference in Springfield, Massachusetts. He wants to stay at a hotel that meets these requirements:

- is near the airport
- has conference rooms
- has a restaurant
- accepts American Express credit cards
- costs no more than $100 a night

He asks you to check the Springfield hotels to find one that meets his needs.

> Directory of United States Hotels   page 38
>
> ### Hotels (Massachusetts)
>
> **Springfield**
> Hudson Hotel, 413-778-0180; Route 32 (2 miles from airport); 100 units, restaurant, conference and meeting rooms available on request, rates $80-100. Credit cards accepted: AmEx, Visa, Master.
> Maple Inn, 413-6236-5780; 174 Main St, 30 units, restaurant open for dinner only, rates $65-85.
> Riverdale Inn, 413-725-9410; 1087 Route 32 (5 miles from center of city); 25 units, pool, sauna, restaurant, rates $80-100. Credit cards accepted: AmEx, Visa, Master.
> Tremont Hotel, 413-225-1725; 51 Port Avenue (downtown Springfield), 116 units, 2 restaurants, conference rooms, rates $90-120. Credit cards accepted: Visa, Master.

What is your purpose for reading this directory?

_____

_____

What services and rooms are available at the Hudson Hotel?

_____

_____

Was Mr. Leto right in thinking that the Hudson Hotel is near the airport? Why?

_____

_____

What are the room rates at the Hudson Hotel? Will they satisfy Mr. Leto?

_____

_____

Work Problem B

Next week Ms. Battista will fly from New York to Los Angeles. She will return to New York on Saturday. She gives you this note:

On Wednesday, I must get to L.A. in time for a 4 P.M. meeting. I think the 10:55 flight from New York looks good. I want a direct flight to L.A. I need an hour to get from the airport to the meeting. I'll take care of my return flight. Please check Amflight in the Airline Directory and check that the 10:55 is the best flight. If another looks better, please let me know. Thanks. Ms. Battista.

Airline Directory				page 7
Amflight Airlines Schedules				
New York—Los Angeles				* = Mon.-Fri. only
Depart NY	Arrive Pittsburgh	Depart Pittsburgh	Arrive LA	Flight No.
8:15 AM	9:45 AM	10:35 AM	12:50 PM	164
9:07 AM			1:20 PM	668*
10:55 AM			3:05 PM	450
12:30 PM			4:25 PM	302
Los Angeles—New York				* = Mon.-Fri. only
Depart LA	Arrive Pittsburgh	Depart Pittsburgh	Arrive NY	Flight No.
11:55 PM	7:25 AM	8:40 AM	9:40 AM	788
12:05 PM			10:05 PM	455*
1:45 PM			11:50 PM	432

What is your purpose for reading this flight information?

_____

_____

Would you recommend that Ms. Battista take the 10:55 flight? Why?

_____

_____

Would flight number 164 satisfy Ms. Battista? Why?

_____

_____

What should you tell Ms. Battista about a return flight to New York?

_____

_____

Work Problem C

You often have to look up information on computer software for Ms. Battista and Mr. Leto. You borrow the Software Users Guide from the company library. Ms. Battista wants to buy a copy for the three of you. She will spend the money because you use it so often. She asks you to make sure it includes the following kinds of information:

- Names and addresses of software producers
- Names and descriptions of programs, including the hardware they run on
- Some sort of subject listing, for example by spreadsheet programs, word processing programs, and so on
- List of user groups

You go to the library and check the guide against Ms. Battista's list. You must then decide how to respond to her.

Software Users Guide   page ii

Contents of Software Users Guide

Software Users Guide   page 156

Spreadsheets

Name of Program: Number Manager

Producer: Syrex Company

Description: This is a spreadsheet program designed for first-time users. Especially good for owners of small businesses. Clear commands, easy to follow. Exceptionally good manual. Not available yet for use on IBM computer.

Hardware: Apple, Epson.

What is your purpose for looking at this guide?

_____

_____

What information do you find in the table of contents to answer Ms. Battista's questions?

_____

_____

What can you tell her about program subject listings in the guide?

_____

_____

What question of Ms. Battista's can you answer by looking on page 156?

_____

_____

Work Problem D

Ms. Battista will include the names of the top agents in the company's annual report. When she does this, she wants each state name to be spelled correctly or the correct abbreviation used. The rules for abbreviation are in the company style manual. She gives you her list of agents and their states.

Top S & G Agents

Leila Ancetta, Col.
Martin Bond, Idaho
Toni DiPace, Ariz.
Alan Golden, Cal.
Edward Harris, Ga.
Roland Luhrs, Alaska
George Morris, Texas
Larry Nestor, Ohio
Judy Richards, Maine
Geoffrey Tomlinson, Utah
Derek Vanderhof, Flor.
Warren Volz, Ala.
Tom Wertheimer, Dela.

S & G Company Official Style Manual   p. 24

Section 4.3—State Names and Abbreviations

Use the two-letter state abbreviations at all times except for the annual report. For the annual report follow the rules below.

1. Do not abbreviate the names of these eight states: Alaska, Hawaii, Idaho, Iowa, Maine, Ohio, Texas, and Utah.

2. Abbreviate the others as follows: Ala., Ariz., Ark., Calif., Colo., Conn., Del., Fla., Ga., Ill., Ind., Kans., Ky., La., Md., Mass., Mich., Minn., Miss., Mo., Mont., Nebr., Nev., N.H., N.J., N.Mex., N.Y., N.C., N.Dak., Okla., Oreg., Pa., R.I., S.C., S.Dak., Tenn., Vt., Va., Wash., W.Va., Wis., Wyo.

What is your purpose for reading this material?

_____

_____

What state names are spelled or abbreviated incorrectly? Write them correctly here.

_____

_____

What state names are spelled or abbreviated correctly?

_____

_____

According the style manual, when would you use two-letter state abbreviations?

_____

_____

Skills Practice: Finding a Word's Meaning

Now let's review some prefixes that you learned in earlier chapters and use them with different root words.

Example: In the Software Users Guide you read this sentence:

This is a spreadsheet program *designed* for first-time users.

Prefix	**(Meaning)**	**Root**
de-	(from, down)	*sign*

A *sign* is an illustration or mark. To *design* means "to draw or mark out." This program was drawn up for use by people new to computers.

Example: You also read this sentence in the lesson:

Ms. Alice Battista wants you to *subscribe* to *Computer Trends* magazine for two years.

Prefix	**(Meaning)**	**Root**
sub-	(under)	*scribe*

Scribe means "to write." To *subscribe* is "to sign an agreement." In this case you agree to pay for a number of issues of the magazine.

Example: In this lesson you read the word *requirements*.

Prefix	**(Meaning)**	**Root**
re-	(again)	*quire*

Quire comes from a word meaning "to ask" or "to seek." *Requirements* are "things that one needs or seeks."

Exercise A

In each sentence below, identify the prefix and the root of the word in italics. Write them in the space below the sentence. Also, write the meaning for the full word. Use both word parts and context to find the meaning.

1. What does that clause of the contract *denote*?

   prefix:_____

   root: _____

   meaning of full word: _____

2. We need to *reserve* early if we want to have a booth at the convention.

prefix:_____

root: _____

meaning of full word: _____

3. Our policies *exclude* smoking in the offices.

prefix:_____

root: _____

meaning of full word: _____

4. The *subsequent* meeting was much better than the first one.

prefix:_____

root: _____

meaning of full word: _____

5. Her *decision* to cancel the contract was clearly premeditated.

prefix:_____

root: _____

meaning of full word: _____

Answers to Skills Practice Exercise A are on page 253.

Exercise B

In each sentence below, identify the prefix and the root of the word in italics. Write them in the space below the sentence. Write the meaning for the full word. Use both word parts and context to find the meaning.

1. Our pride in our company *derives* from many years of providing good service.

prefix:_____

root: _____

meaning of full word: _____

2. I will *request* that my boss give me a raise.

prefix:_____

root: _____

meaning of full word: _____

3. We are *expanding* our line of products.

prefix:_____

root: _____

meaning of full word: _____

4. Our heavy work schedule *precludes* our taking on more work at this time.

prefix:_____

root: _____

meaning of full word: _____

5. We were *detained* at the office by the heavy workload.

prefix:_____

root: _____

meaning of full word: _____

Check Yourself

Work Problem

Ms. Ruis is planning a two-day workshop at the River Hotel and Conference Center. She wants to reserve a meeting room for fifteen to twenty people. She will also need an overhead projector and an easel in the room. Many people attending the workshop will not have cars, so there must be several restaurants in the Center.

Mrs. Ruis asks you to check the hotel directory to see if the Center can meet all her needs. She also wants you to see if there are phone numbers to call for reserving the conference room and making a dinner reservation.

Directory of United States Hotels   page 208

River Hotel and Conference Center

Located twenty miles from downtown Hartsville on the beautiful Randel River.

The River Hotel is given an A+ rating by the ABA Travel Guide and the American Hotel Association. The Conference Center has been in operation for over twenty years.

It was the site of a major U.S.-Korean conference. Many people traveling from other countries plan business meetings at the Center. The staff is well prepared to handle the needs of the international traveler.

The conference rooms are excellent. They can accommodate from five to 250 people. The staff can supply a wide variety of equipment including computers, overhead projectors, copiers, easels, microphones, and podiums. Call the conference manager, Will Sikes, for more information (203-787-9991).

See the table on page 312 for room rates and a map. For room reservations call 203-787-9990.

The Hotel has five excellent restaurants ranging from the casual Sunshine Room to the formal River Lounge. The Sunshine Room is open from 5:30 A.M. to 10:00 PM. The River Lounge is open for dinner only. Call the restaurant manager for more information (203-787-9994).

Exercise

As you read, try to decide the meaning of any difficult words you find from the sentence or paragraph in which they appear. Read each sentence below. Circle the letter before the word that most closely matches the word in italics.

1. What kind of *operation* do you have?

    a) cooperation
    b) computer
    c) business
    d) information

2. We have a loyal *clientele*.

   a) number of cars in the parking lot
   b) customers
   c) patients
   d) organizers

3. We will be able to *accommodate* your needs.

   a) hold, serve
   b) check out
   c) telephone
   d) watch

4. We think you will find that our *facilities* will fit your needs.

   a) places for specific purposes
   b) parking lots
   c) road service
   d) maps and guidebooks

5. We have *exclusive* rights in this area.

   a) unshared
   b) outside
   c) inside
   d) quiet

Now consider your work problem and the directory page you are reading. Answer the following questions. Remember to define, plan, read, and check.

What is your purpose for reading this directory page?

_____

_____

What are Ms. Ruis's needs for a meeting room? Can the Center meet them?

_____

_____

What are Ms. Ruis's needs for restaurants? Can the Center meet them?

_____

_____

What phone numbers do you give Ms. Ruis to reserve the conference room and a table for dinner?

_____

_____

Answers to Problem-Solving Practice Questions

Define Your Problem

What is my purpose for reading this material?

To check subscription information.

What should I be able to do when I finish reading?

Tell Ms. Battista subscription cost and whether two rates.

Plan Your Solution

What information do I need from this material to solve my work problem?

Cost of subscription and rate information.

How carefully will I have to read to find the information I need?

Carefully, watching for subscription information and city where magazine published.

Read

What information do the format clues give me?

Addresses and rates.

What do I already know about this situation that will help me?

There may be two magazines with same name. One I need is in California.

Should I continue reading this material?

Yes, to find out about subscription rates.

What information is important because it helps me solve my work problem?

Subscription information and city of publication.

Have I checked the new information against original information?

Yes.

Check Your Solution

Did I accomplish my purpose? (Was I able to check the information?)

Yes.

Did the information help me solve my work problem? How?

Yes. I found the information that Ms. Battista wanted.

Answers to Skills Practice Exercise A

1. prefix: *de-*
   root: *note*
   meaning of full word: "mean"
2. prefix: *re-*
   root: *serve*
   meaning of full word: "to keep or get for oneself"
3. prefix: *ex-*
   root: *clude*
   meaning of full word: "ban, prevent"
4. prefix: *sub-*
   root: *sequent*
   meaning of full word: "later"
5. prefix: *de-*
   root: *cision*
   meaning of full word: "choice, vote, selection"

Putting It All Together

You are back at your job as an intern at MailMart. Remember that this large firm sells clothing and sporting goods throughout the country. It sells mostly through catalogs. It also runs a large store that people visit from all over. As an intern learning the business, you are required to work in many different jobs.

Work Problem A

Darcie Turner says, "Here's a page from our new fall catalog. Most of our business comes from catalog sales so it must be accurate. All the items and the prices must be in the catalog exactly as we agreed at our March meeting." Ms. Turner says, "Please make sure they are."

Look at the reading material at the end of the unit. Find the pages that contain the information you need to check. Read them. Then answer the following questions.

Which pages did you select to read?

_____

_____

What is your purpose for reading these materials?

_____

_____

List any missing items.

_____

_____

Do you see any price differences? What are they?

_____

_____

What can you tell Ms. Turner after you have checked the two lists?

_____

_____

Work Problem B

Ms. Turner reminds you of Juan Cortez. She says, "He's a great customer, but we made some mistakes on recent orders we sent him. If we get this next order wrong, he'll stop doing business with us. I don't want that to happen."

She says, "His new order has been prepared by the shipping department. I want you to double-check it before it goes." She asks you to check the invoice with Mr. Cortez's order. If there are any differences, you must stop the shipment and let her know right away.

Look at the invoices and purchase orders at the end of the unit. Pick the ones with the information you need to check. Read them. Then answer the following questions.

Which documents did you select to read?

_____

_____

In your own words, give your reasons for reading these documents.

_____

_____

Do you think the order is OK to ship according to the invoice, or do you see things that would cause you to stop the shipment?

_____

_____

What reasons would you give Ms. Turner for stopping the shipment?

_____

_____

DATE: March 4, 199—

FROM: Israel Rojas, General Manager

TO: All Department Managers

SUBJECT: FALL CATALOG MEETING

This is to notify all department managers of the Fall Catalog Meeting. This is an important meeting to prepare the fall catalog. All managers must attend.

The meeting will be held March 18 beginning at 8:30 a.m. in the conference room. The meeting, as usual, will last all day. Please be sure to mark your calendars.

In addition to the usual items, we will discuss the following new items and prices to be included in the fall catalog. If we all agree, these will go in the catalog.

Item	Price
Crewneck Ragg Sweaters	
Men's Regular Dyed	$29.50
Men's Regular Gray	$25.50
Women's Dyed	$29.50
Women's Gray	$25.50
Shawl Collar Ragg Sweaters	
Men's Regular Dyed	$35.00
Men's Regular Gray	$32.00
Women's Dyed	$35.00
Women's Gray	$32.00
Plaid Shirts	
Men's Regular	$21.50
Men's Tall	$23.00
Women's	$21.00
Stretch Denim Jeans	
Men's	$35.00
Women's	$35.00

Thank you and see you at the meeting.

MAILMART Purchase Order Form

ORDERED BY:

Juan Cortez
1122 High Street
Coventry, RI 02816

GIFT ORDER SHIP TO:

Marc Cortez
3302 Middle Road
East Greenwich, RI 01818

Page	Stock No.	Color	Size	How Many	Description	Amount
33	3028	Blue	15½	2	Oxford Cloth Shirt	46.00
33	3029	White	15½	4	Oxford Cloth Shirt	92.00
73	8811			1	Cycling Computer	41.00

PAYMENT METHOD:		Item total	
CREDIT CARD NO.	_____	Regular shipping free	179.00
AMOUNT ENCLOSED	_____	Express shipping	$8.75
BILL SENDER	_____	TOTAL:	187.75

Special instructions:

As you can see, this order must be sent to Marc Cortez, not to me. I want it shipped express service to arrive in time for his birthday. Thank you.

MAILMART FALL CATALOG

SWEATERS

Item	Price
Crewneck Ragg Sweaters	
Men's Regular Dyed	$29.50
Men's Regular Gray	$29.50
Women's Dyed	$29.50
Women's Gray	$25.50
Shawl Collar Ragg Sweaters	
Men's Regular Dyed	$45.00
Women's Dyed	$35.00
Women's Gray	$32.00

SHIRTS

Item	Price
Plaid Shirts	
Men's Regular	$21.50
Men's Tall	$23.00

JEANS

Item	Price
Stretch Denim Jeans Men's	$35.00
Stretch Denim Jeans Women's	$36.00

MailMart **Invoice**				123 Lake Road Detroit, MI 48200 Tel: 313-444-3333 Fax: 313-555-5555	
Ship to:	Juan Cortez 1122 High Street Coventry, RI 02816				
Bill to:	Marc Cortez 3302 Middle Road East Greenwich, RI 01818				
	Date Shipped: 3/18/9–			Ship Via: Reg.Mail	
Item No.	Description	Color	Size	Quantity	Unit Price	Cost
3028 3028 8811	Oxford cloth shirt Oxford cloth shirt Cycling computer	Blue White	15 1/2 15 1/2	2 4 1	$23.00 23.00 41.00	$46.00 92.00 41.00
					Subtotal:	$179.00
					Shipping:	Free
					Sales Tax:	
					Total Due:	$179.00
Please enclose yellow copy with payment.						

UNIT IV

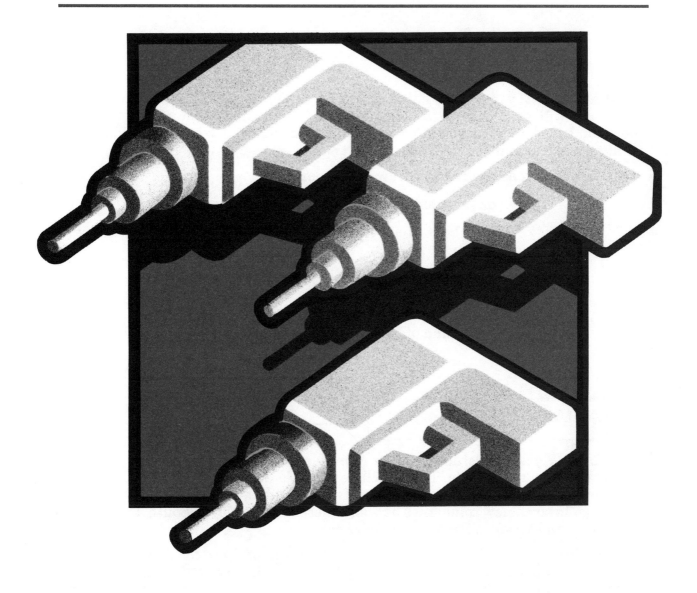

READING TO
DRAW CONCLUSIONS

In the last unit, you read to check new information against existing information. Now you will read to draw conclusions. To draw a conclusion means to make a decision based on what you have read. It also means that you have to take action that no one has told you take.

Do the following as you read to draw conclusions:

1. Look for information that the format provides.

2. Think about what you already know about this situation that will help you.

3. Decide whether to continue reading the material.

4. Pick out the information that helps you solve your work problem.

5. Put new and old information together to draw a conclusion.

Major Manufacturing Company

In Unit IV you will return to Major Manufacturing Company where you will meet several new people. These include Amy Ho in the customer service department, Elie Rodin, sales manager, and Lewis Randall, personnel director. You will go to some new companies as well. These include North-South Travel Agency and Western Secretarial Services.

In addition, you will work at Enterprise Department Store for Elena Del Santos, the manager. You will meet people in various departments, such as the customer service manager, the toy and hat department managers, and the safety officer.

You will end the unit at Mailmart with Fred Montoya, who is in charge of the accounting department.

LESSON 13

Reading Letters and Memos to Draw Conclusions

As you become more experienced in your job, you will often be asked to draw your own conclusions. You will put together different pieces of information to decide what to do.

Reading to Draw Conclusions

Amy Ho works in the customer service department at Major Manufacturing Company. Recently she was promoted to supervisor. She is proud that her department handles orders so well. One day she receives a letter from a customer with a complaint. Look at the letter to see how Amy reads it to draw conclusions.

1. She looks for information from the format clues. (It is a letter from Elwin Janus of M & R.)

2. She looks for what she already knows about the situation that will help her. (She knows that Mr. Janus has been a customer of Major for a long time because she has handled orders from him.)

3. She decides whether to continue reading the letter. (Yes, she wants to find out what the letter is about so she can decide what to do about it.)

4. She picks out the information that helps her solve her work problem. (His last three orders have been late, and he is frustrated by Major's service.)

5. She puts the new and the old information together to draw a conclusion. (She decides to pay special attention to Janus's next few orders so they are handled right and Major does not lose a good customer.)

Elwin Janus
M & R Home Heating Company
18 Water Street, Alton, IL 62002

February 22, 199-

Major Manufacturing Company
181 Gorham Road
Alton, IL 62002

Dear Customer Service:

This is the third time I have written to complain about late shipments. I always ask to have my orders shipped by overnight delivery. Please check my last two orders. One was ten days late.

I have been a customer of Major for 20 years and do not want to stop doing business with you. There are other places I could go to, but I like your products. I'm sure you do not want to lose my business. I buy over $20,000 worth of products from you each year.

Please give me better service on my next order.

Elwin Janus

263

Amy read to draw conclusions. Before reading, she used the problem-solving strategy. Let's go through another work problem using this strategy.

Work Problem

Ms. Clive is on vacation and will return on June 26. She is meeting with a major customer from 10:00 to 11:00 A.M. the day she returns. You know she will want to spend the rest of the day catching up on paperwork.

While she is away, you read Ms. Clive's mail for anything that needs immediate action. The following memo comes in from Pat O'Toole, Ms. Clive's boss.

```
DATE:     June 20, 199-

TO:       Roberta Clive, Angela Qwan

FROM:     Pat O'Toole

RE:       WORK SHIFTS

I would like to get together with
both of you to discuss rescheduling
some work shifts.  With summer
vacations coming up, we must be
sure adequate customer service
staff is on duty at all times.

I would like to meet at 10:30 on
June 26.  If this is not good for
you, I can easily do it later.
Just suggest another time and date.
However, we must meet this month.

Please call or have your assistant
call about this before June 24.
```

Define Your Problem

What is my purpose for reading this material?

To conclude whether memo needs immediate action.

What should I be able to do when I finish reading?

Take action or let memo wait until Ms. Clive returns.

Plan Your Solution

What information do I need from this material to solve my work problem?

To find out if Ms. Clive's manager needs anything before the 26th.

How carefully will I have to read to find the information I need?

Carefully for details about writer's needs.

Read

What information do the format clues give me?

This is a memo from Ms. Clive's boss.

What do I already know about this situation that will help me?

Ms. Clive has important meeting on 26th and may not want to schedule other meetings that day.

Should I continue reading this material?

Yes. There is a problem that I may have to act on.

What information is important because it helps me solve my work problem?

Ms. O'Toole wants to meet on the 26th but says it can be another day if necessary.

Have I put the new and old information together and decided what to do?

Yes. Call Ms. O'Toole, explain the problem, and say anytime on 27th would be OK.

Check Your Solution

Did I accomplish my purpose? (Did I draw a conclusion and make a decision?)

Yes.

Did the information help me solve my work problem? How?

Yes. I have responded to Ms. O'Toole's memo on time with information she needs.

Problem-Solving Practice

Now apply your strategy to another work problem.

Work Problem

Roberta Clive is organizing a workshop to train new customer service staff. She has received a letter from Lake Erie Center, a possible place to have the workshop.

Ms. Clive tells you, "Read this letter and compare it with the one in the file from Niagara Center. Tell me which one you think would be better to work with. And remember, we must choose a place that is easy to get to."

**Lake Erie Center
2206 14th Avenue, Buffalo, NY 14200**

September 12, 199-

Roberta Clive
American Turbine, Inc.
3434 Mohawk Road
Buffalo, NY 14200

Dear Ms. Clive:

I am in receipt of your letter of September 3. Here is the information you asked for. We are on the third street east of First Avenue. We are one hour from the airport and about 20 minutes from the Falls Shopping Center. I don't know where that is in relation to your location on Mohawk Road.

Our rate for a full day includes a lunch. The lunch consists of an entree (choice of two), a salad, a beverage, and dessert. I can give you a quote for a group meeting.

Sincerely,

Maria Matthews
Administrative Assistant

Niagara Center
36 Lake Parkway
Niagara Falls, NY 14300

September 8, 199-

Roberta Clive
American Turbine, Inc.
3434 Mohawk Road
Buffalo, NY 14200

Dear Ms. Clive:

Thank you for your letter of September 3. We are in the city of Niagara Falls, only 45 minutes from downtown Buffalo. I have enclosed a map and have marked on it the route you would follow from Mohawk Road. If you need directions from other places, I would be glad to help you.

We will be happy to meet with you to discuss your requirements for conference rooms and meals. Please call me at your convenience (718-554-8472). We can send a representative to your office. We will try to oblige you in any way we can.

Sincerely,

A.L. Rondo
General Manager

Define Your Problem

What is my purpose for reading this material?

_____

_____

What should I be able to do when I finish reading?

_____

_____

Plan Your Solution

What information do I need from this
material to solve my work problem?

_____

_____

_____

_____

How carefully will I have to read to find
the information I need?

_____

_____

_____

Read

What information do the format clues
give me?

_____

_____

_____

_____

What do I already know about this
situation that will help me?

_____

_____

_____

_____

Should I continue reading this material?

_____

_____

_____

_____

What information is important because it helps me solve my work problem?

_____

_____

_____

_____

Have I put the new and old information together and decided what to do?

_____

_____

_____

Check Your Solution

Did I accomplish my purpose? (Did I draw a conclusion and make a decision?)

_____

_____

_____

_____

Did the information help me solve my work problem? How?

_____

_____

_____

_____

Answers to the Problem-Solving Practice questions are on pages 282-283.

On Your Own

Now you will work through four more problems in which you read memos and letters to draw conclusions. Remember to define your purpose and plan your solution. Read and, if you need to, reread some or all of the documents carefully. Finally, check to see if you have solved your problem.

Work Problem A

Several days ago you received a memo from the shipping department. The shipping crew says the shipping cartons are not sturdy. Sometimes cartons come apart as the crew is packing them. The crew feels that the cartons are not strong enough for mailing the company's products.

Today you received the letter shown here.

August 16, 199-

Major Manufacturing Company
181 Gorham Road
Alton, IL 62002

Dear Major Manufacturing Company:

The power drill that I ordered from you arrived yesterday. Its carton was torn in five places. The handle was sticking out of the carton and had three dents in it.

I would like to return it for an undamaged drill. I think I should receive a product that is intact.

Please send the new drill in a better carton. The one you used this time was not up to the job.

Sincerely,

John Jasper

How can this letter help you solve your work problem?

_____

_____

What information in this letter is important when compared with the memo from the shipping department?

_____

_____

Could the damaged carton be the result of rough handling by the post office? Why?

_____

_____

Besides handling Mr. Jasper's complaint, what do you think you should do?

_____

_____

Work Problem B

You are an agent at North-South Travel Agency. You are making arrangements for your client, Mr. Arnold, to spend a vacation in Mexico. He wants to stay one night in Mexico City. He does not want to spend more than $80 for a room but would like a hotel with a pool. There are several wonderful restaurants where he hopes to eat. So far, you have not found a hotel at this price that you would recommend. This letter arrives from a North-South agent in Florida.

North-South Travel
4321 Royal Palm Drive
Miami, FL 33100

March 28, 199-

North-South Travel
792 Jarrel Avenue
St. Louis, MO 63100

Dear (your name):

I have just been to Mexico City and stayed at a delightful little hotel. It is the Amigo and is on a quiet street in the center of the city. The owner wants to encourage people to visit the city as a vacation spot. There are some excellent restaurants nearby.

The owner is offering a special deal: stay two nights for $70 each, and get two meals at local restaurants for half price.

Regular room rates start at $90 a night. I think this is a real bargain. The hotel is charming and the restaurants on the owner's list are all superb. The hotel, of course, has a pool. I stayed there for four days and found it very relaxing.

Sincerely,

Kelly Rhee, Agent

How can this letter help you solve your work problem?

_____

_____

How much does Mr. Arnold want to spend for one night in a hotel? How does that compare with the Amigo price?

_____

_____

Give three reasons why Mr. Arnold might like to stay at the Amigo Hotel.

_____

_____

What recommendation will you make to Mr. Arnold? Explain your answer.

_____

_____

Work Problem C

Ms. Khan wants to buy a new copier for the office. She says it must have certain features. It should be able to
- enlarge and reduce
- take legal size paper
- handle large quantities quickly
- sort

Quality Equipment has sent information on its copiers. Ms. Khan says, "Please read this and tell me if one of the Quality Equipment copiers fits our needs."

Quality Equipment
3 Canal Street, Williamsport, WA 98795

April 6, 199-

Anna Khan
Western Secretarial Services
14 Hopewell Road
Williamsport, WA 98795

Dear Ms. Khan:

In answer to your letter, we suggest one of the following three copiers:

Model #233. This model can enlarge and reduce the original. It also takes legal size paper (10 x 14). Its copy speed is about five pages a minute. This is our most cost effective model.

Next we have the Model #333. This has an automatic feeder for making large numbers of copies quickly. It copies up to nine pages a minute. It also has a five-bin sorter. Of course, it takes legal-size paper and can enlarge and reduce. This model is in the middle price range and is an excellent buy.

Our most expensive model is the #433. It has exceptional features if you are willing to pay the price. It is very fast—22 copies a minute. It can print in four colors, and it does everything the other two copiers do.

Please let me know if any of these fits your requirements. I would be glad to discuss prices with you. I look forward to hearing from you.

Yours truly,

Bill Plato, Sales

How can this letter help you solve your work problem?

_____

_____

Does Model #233 have all the features that Ms. Khan wants? List any that it does not have.

_____

_____

Does Model #433 have any features that Ms. Khan does not want? List them.

_____

_____

Which model should you recommend to Ms. Khan? Why did you choose it?

_____

_____

Work Problem D

Ms. Khan is away for three days at the Seattle office. She is meeting people there to discuss the new office in Oregon. They are considering two possible locations for the new office. Ms. Khan wants you to call if any important mail comes in while she is away.

Pacific Real Estate
48 Oregon Avenue
Portland, Oregon 97200

April 14, 199-

Anna Khan
Western Secretarial Services
14 Hopewell Road
Williamsport, WA 98795

Dear Ms. Khan:

I just received some important information about the site in the Mountain Shopping Mall in Portland. This is the one you are considering for your new office. The owner is willing to reduce his price by about ten percent. He would like an answer as soon as possible because several other people are also interested in it. Please call me as soon as you can at (503) 642-1357.

By the way, the site you rejected on Route 402 has just been rented. I am sure you do not regret your decision. It was not as attractive as the mall site.

Yours truly,

Ed Rice

How can this letter help you solve your work problem?

_____

_____

What important information from this letter might Ms. Khan want to have while she is in Seattle?

_____

_____

What information can wait until Ms. Khan gets back?

_____

_____

Do you decide to call Ms. Khan? If you call, what do you tell her?

_____

_____

Skills Practice: Finding a Word's Meaning

Being able to determine a new word's meaning from its context is a valuable skill in the business world. Practice your skill with the following exercises.

Example: In the letter to Roberta Clive from Maria Matthews, you saw this sentence:

> *I am in receipt* of your letter of September 3.

This is another way of saying, "I have your letter." This expression is sometimes used in business letters.

Example: In the same letter, you saw this:

> I can give you a *quote* for a group meeting.

Quote can mean

1. someone else's words
2. price or bid

In this case, it means, "I can give you a *price* for a group meeting."

Exercise A

Read the following sentences. On the blank lines below each sentence, write what the word in italics means based on the sentence it is in.

1. The map shows the best *thoroughfare* to take from here to downtown.

   _____

2. I was comfortable at this hotel. It has much better *accommodations* than the other one.

   _____

3. We are now using a different kind of shipping carton that is more *durable* than the old one.

   _____

4. They take very good care of the copier so it is always in *optimum* working condition.

   _____

5. This product is damaged. Please send a new one that is *intact*.

   _____

Answers to Skills Practice Exercise A are on page 283.

Exercise B

Read the following sentences. On the blank line following each, write what the word in italics means based on the sentence it is in.

1. This customer is angry because of late shipments. Please try to *expedite* his next order.

_____

2. I like what this store has to sell, but I like the *wares* in the other one better.

_____

3. To *requisition* a new copier, you will have to get the approval at of least two top-level managers.

_____

4. All the major office buildings are downtown in what is known as the *commercial* center.

_____

5. The travel agency started out small but has grown to be an *enterprise* with over ten offices throughout the state.

_____

Check Yourself

Work Problem

Ms. Khan wants you to order paper for the copier. She called Brice Paper Company and asked for a quote on thirty reams of white twenty-pound paper for the copier and for letters. She does not want to pay more than $250 plus shipping and taxes. You read the letter from Brice when it comes in.

Brice Paper Company
30 Walton Street, Seattle, WA 98009

May 13, 199–

Anna Khan
Western Secretarial Services
14 Hopewell Road
Williamsport, WA 98795

Dear Ms. Khan:

I am pleased to give you a quote on 30 reams of our quality White Foam paper. It is excellent for use in duplicating machines and for correspondence. It comes in 16-pound, 20-pound, and 22-pound weight.

Thirty reams of 8.5 x 11 20-pound weight cost $270, plus shipping and tax. Shipping for normal delivery is about $10. Express service is extra.

Please call us at our toll-free number. We will dispatch your order immediately. We look forward to accommodating you.

Yours truly,

Randy Brice
Brice Paper Co.

Exercise

Before solving the work problem, try to decide the meaning of following words. Choose the right meaning from the choices below.

1. ream

        a) a package containing paper bags
        b) a package containing 500 sheets of paper
        c) a special shipping carton
        d) special printing ink

2. duplicating machines

      a) slot machines
      b) computers
      c) copiers
      d) printers

3. dispatch

      a) send
      b) receive
      c) lose
      d) ignore

4. express

      a) slower
      b) better
      c) faster
      d) wider

5. accommodate

      a) write
      b) talk to
      c) set a date
      d) serve

Now consider your work problem and the decision you must make. Answer the following questions. Remember to define, plan, read, and check.

How can this letter help you solve your work problem?

_____

_____

What information does the letter give about the kind of paper that Ms. Khan wants to order?

_____

_____

What price does the paper company offer? How does the price compare with Ms. Khan's needs?

_____

_____

Do you decide to order the paper? Why?

_____

_____

Answers To Problem-Solving Practice Questions

Define Your Problem

What is my purpose for reading this material?

Decide which is the better place for the workshop.

What should I be able to do when I finish reading?

Make a recommendation to Ms. Clive.

Plan Your Solution

What information do I need from this material to solve my work problem?

Which center will be better to work with and easier to get to.

How carefully will I have to read to find the information I need?

Carefully, to compare information on each location.

Read

What information do the format clues give me?

Who sent the letters and when.

What do I already know about this situation that will help me?

The place I recommend must be easy to get to.

Should I continue reading this material?

Yes, until I can make a decision.

What information is important because it helps me solve my work problem?

One place sends a map and letter that indicates they want to be helpful.

Have I put the new and old information together and decided what to do?

Yes. Recommend Niagara Center.

Check Your Solution

Did I accomplish my purpose? (Did I draw a conclusion and make a decision?)

Yes.

Did the information help me solve my work problem? How?

Yes. I will recommend Niagara because they enclosed map and because letter is more helpful.

Answers To Skills Practice Exercise A

1. *thoroughfare* means "road"
2. *accommodations* means "room and meals"
3. *durable* means "strong"
4. *optimum* means "the best"
5. *intact* means "whole"

LESSON 14

Reading Forms to Draw Conclusions

One advantage of a form is that only important information is included. You do not have to read long paragraphs to understand what is being ordered or requested. Still, you must be able to look at a form and draw a conclusion about the information on it. Is it something you must act on? Is it a request for information or supplies? Is the information in the form correct?

Reading to Draw Conclusions

Chris Harrison works at the Enterprise Department Store for Ms. Elena Del Santos. Ms. Del Santos asks Chris to interview people who applied for the job of night manager. Chris must compare information on the job application forms with information in the job description. The job description says a night manager must have
- a technical school degree
- three years of experience in store management

Chris must separate the applications into two groups: qualified and unqualified. She must set up appointments for those who qualify. Look at the job application from Michael Robinson and see how Chris Harrison reads it to draw conclusions.

Enterprise Department Store
Employment Application

Date _Feb. 8, 199–_   Telephone _914-555-6731_

Name _Michael Robinson_

Address _54 Water Street_

City/State/Zip _Lawrence, KS   66044_

Position Wanted _Night Manager_

Education

High School

Central High School, 198–

College

Associate Degree of General Studies
Kansas Technical Institute, June 8, 199–

Experience

Place _Dairy Mart_   Dates _7/91 to 12/91_

Position _Assistant Manager_

Place _Dairy Mart_   Dates _7/89 to 7/91_

Position _Cashier_

Place _Quality Variety Stores_ Dates _1/88 to 6/89_

Position _Warehouse Stock Clerk_

References

Walter Fry, Manager, Dairy Mart

1. She looks for information from the format clues. (The applicant's name, address, phone, education, and job experience.)

2. She looks for what she already knows about the situation that will help her. (An application form lists a person's experience and education. She knows the job requirements.)

3. She decides whether to continue reading this material. (Yes, to decide whether to set up appointment.)

4. She picks out the information that helps her solve her work problem. (He has a technical school degree. He does not have three years of managerial experience.)

5. She puts the new and the old information together to draw a conclusion. (His qualifications do not match all those in the job description. She does not need to set up an appointment.)

Work Problem

You are helping Chris Harrison check the applications. You look at the next one.

Enterprise Department Store
Employment Application

Date _Feb. 10, 199–_   Telephone _914-555-0087_

Name _Betsy Tan_

Address _1825 Elm Lane_

City/State/Zip _Lawrence, KS 66044_

Position Wanted _Night Manager_

Education

High School

Central High School, 198–

College

_____

_____

Experience

Place _Dora's Dress Shop_ Dates _6/89 to 6/91_

Position _Weekend Manager_

Place _Charlie's Chicken & Deli_ Dates _1/88 to 6/89_

Position _Assistant Night Manager_

Place _____ Dates _____

Position _____

References

Dora Ritter, Owner, Dora's Dress Shop

_____

_____

Define Your Problem

What is my purpose for reading this material?

To decide whether to set up appointment with applicant.

What should I be able to do when I finish reading?

Know if B. Tan's background matches job description.

Plan Your Solution

What information do I need from this material to solve my work problem?

Applicant's education and experience.

How carefully will I have to read to find the information I need?

Skim first few lines. Then read carefully for education and experience.

Read

What information do the format clues give me?

Each section requests specific information as indicated by the headings.

What do I already know about this situation that will help me?

Job requires technical school degree and 3 years' experience as a manager.

Should I continue reading this material?

Yes, to find out if person has necessary background.

What information is important because it helps me solve my work problem?

This person does not have necessary degree or experience.

Have I put the new and old information together and decided what to do?

Yes. Compare job description (old) with application form (new). Do not make appointment.

Check Your Solution

Did I accomplish my purpose? (Did I draw a conclusion and make a decision?)

Yes. Person does not have needed background for job.

Did the information help me solve my work problem? How?

Yes. I do not set up interview with applicant.

Problem-Solving Practice

Now apply your strategy to another work problem.

Work Problem

Elena Del Santos is out of town for several days. While she is away, the assistant manager, Thomas Monroe, is in charge. He has asked you to keep him informed of any messages that he should know about.

When you return from lunch, you find the following message in Ms. Del Santos's in-box.

For _Elena Del Santos_

Date _2/15_ Time _12:30_

WHILE YOU WERE OUT

M _Frank_

From _B.J. Shipping Co._

Phone No. _817_ _555_ _7171_
Area Code Number Extension

TELEPHONED		URGENT	
PLEASE CALL		WANTS TO SEE YOU	
WILL CALL AGAIN		CAME TO SEE YOU	
RETURNED YOUR CALL			

Message _The shipment from Texas has been delayed because of bad weather. It should be there by noon Tuesday._

_R.B._
Operator

Define Your Problem

What is my purpose for reading this material?

_____

_____

What should I be able to do when I finish reading?

_____

_____

Plan Your Solution

What information do I need from this material to solve my work problem?

_____

_____

_____

_____

How carefully will I have to read to find the information I need?

_____

_____

_____

Read

What information do the format clues give me?

_____

_____

_____

_____

What do I already know about this situation that will help me?

_____

_____

_____

_____

Should I continue reading this material?

_____

_____

What information is important because
it helps me solve my work problem?

_____

_____

_____

_____

Have I put the new and old information
together and decided what to do?

_____

_____

_____

Check Your Solution

Did I accomplish my purpose? (Did I draw
a conclusion and make a decision?)

_____

_____

_____

_____

Did the information help me solve my
work problem? How?

_____

_____

_____

_____

Answers to the Problem-Solving Practice questions are on pages 301-303.

On Your Own

Now read four more business forms to draw conclusions. Remember to define your purpose and plan your solution before you read. If you need to, reread some or all of the forms carefully. Finally, check to see that you have solved your problem.

Work Problem A

Enterprise Department Store is known for selling good products at good prices. Customer service is its weak point. Customer service manager Warren Long gave six weeks of training to all employees. He also gave out Customer Service Rating Forms to all customers.

He is now reviewing the completed forms to see if his work is a success. He has asked you to decide if the comments on one form should be discussed with the store manager.

CUSTOMER SERVICE RATING FORM

Thank you for shopping at Enterprise Department Store. Please take a moment to fill out the form below. Your comments and suggestions will help us improve our service. Circle the answer or number that best reflects your experience. 1 is a low rating and 5 is a high rating.

OVERALL, HOW PLEASANT WAS YOUR SHOPPING EXPERIENCE?

| 1 | 2 | 3 | (4) | 5 |

WERE THE ITEMS YOU WANTED IN STOCK?

NO   (YES)

HOW WOULD YOU RATE OUR

HELPFULNESS?

| 1 | 2 | 3 | (4) | 5 |

COURTESY?

| 1 | 2 | 3 | (4) | 5 |

KNOWLEDGE OF OUR PRODUCTS?

| 1 | 2 | (3) | 4 | 5 |

PROMPTNESS OF SERVICE?

| 1 | (2) | 3 | 4 | 5 |

COMMENTS OR SUGGESTIONS: *My experience was mostly good. But in the check-out line I had to wait 5 minutes behind a person paying with a check. Why don't you have an express line for people who pay with cash?*

How can this form help you solve your work problem?

_____

_____

How would you rate this customer's feeling about the store?

_____

_____

What suggestion does the customer make? Does it seem worth passing along to the manager? Why?

_____

_____

Work Problem B

Elena Del Santos is the manager of Enterprise Department Store. She knows how unhappy customers are when sale items are not available. One company, PreSchool Puzzles, frequently fails to send stock in time for announced sales. Its shipments are sometimes misdirected.

Ms. Del Santos has decided to remove the puzzles from the sales ad if enough puzzles are not received. The toy department manager, Barbara Collins, says that she will need at least 150 puzzles for the sale.

Ms. Del Santos and Ms. Collins ask you to look at today's shipment. They want you to decide if puzzles will be part of the sale this week. You look at the packing slip for the shipment.

PreSchool Puzzles Packing Slip	435 Hatchett Mill Road Minneapolis, MN 55406 Tel: 612-555-2222 Fax: 612-111-5555		
Ship to: Enterprise Department Store Gateway Shopper's Mall Lawrence, KA 66044	DATE ENTERED 2/15/199–		
Date Shipped: 2/27/9–			
Item No.	Description	Quantity Ordered	Quantity Shipped	Back Ordered
PO40031	Pets Puzzle	50	5	45
TO76009	Tools Puzzle	50	0	50
MM65008	Mickey Mouse Puzzle	50	13	37
TO90087	Train Puzzle	50	0	50
CR20006	Crayons Puzzle	50	25	25

How can this form help you solve your work problem?

_____

_____

How many puzzles did the store order? How many puzzles did the store receive?

_____

_____

Is the number of puzzles the store received enough for the sale? Why?

_____

_____

Work Problem C

Enterprise Department Store still has no night manager. Elena Del Santos interviewed the initial (first) group of people, but she did not find the right person for the job.

She has decided that a degree is nonessential. Management experience is more important. She asks you to review the applications of the people who were not interviewed. What do you decide about this applicant?

Enterprise Department Store
Employment Application

Date _Feb. 10, 199-_   Telephone _914-555-0087_

Name _Betsy Tan_

Address _1825 Elm Lane_

City/State/Zip _Lawrence, KS   66044_

Position Wanted _Night Manager_

Education

High School

Central High School, 198-

College

_____

_____

Experience

Place _Dora's Dress Shop_ Dates _6/89 to 6/91_

Position _Weekend Manager_

Place _Charlie's Chicken & Deli_ Dates _1/88 to 6/89_

Position _Assistant Night Manager_

Place _____ Dates _____

Position _____

References

Dora Ritter, Owner, Dora's Dress Shop

_____

_____

How can this application help you solve your work problem?

_____

_____

Why was this person not interviewed before?

_____

_____

What new information changes your reaction to this person's application?

_____

_____

What do you decide to do?

_____

_____

Work Problem D

Overtime pay at Enterprise Department Store has been increasing over the last two months. Elena Del Santos asks Vera Monte to see if she can detect why this is happening. Vera studies the time sheets for the past two months.

The only group of employees going over the budget is the cashiers. A cashier will always work overtime if another cashier is late. This is expensive. Vera asks you to review the time sheets for each cashier to find the problem.

TIME SHEET

Name _____

Week Ending _____

Shift _____

DAY	IN	OUT	TOTAL HRS
SUN			
MON			
TUE			
WED			
THU			
FRI			
SAT			

How can this document help you solve your work problem?

_____

_____

How many times has Dorothy Lord been late?

_____

_____

What conclusion can you draw from Dorothy's timesheet?

_____

_____

Have you solved your work problem? Why?

_____

_____

Skills Practice: Finding a Word's Meaning

Here are more prefixes that you may find in business situations.

Example: Earlier, you read this sentence.

Its shipments are *misdirected.*

Prefix	**(Meaning)**	**Root**
mis-	wrong	*direct*

Misdirected means "being sent to the wrong place."

Example: Earlier, you also read this sentence.

She has decided that a college degree is *nonessential.*

Prefix	**(Meaning)**	**Root**
non-	(not)	*essential*

Essential means "required." Thus *nonessential* means "not required."

Exercise A

Read the following sentences. On the blank lines following each sentence, write the prefix and root of the word in italics. Then write what the word means based on your knowledge of the prefix and the root.

1. The monthly sales figures show a *decrease* from last month's figures.

   prefix:_____

   root: _____

   meaning of full word: _____

2. Most rumors at work are simply sources of *misinformation.*

   prefix:_____

   root: _____

   meaning of full word: _____

3. Martin informed the customer that the smooth surface would be scratched unless it was cleaned carefully with a *nonabrasive* cleanser.

prefix:_____

root: _____

meaning of full word: _____

4. Vera was able to *detect* why the company was spending so much on overtime.

prefix:_____

root: _____

meaning of full word: _____

5. Please clean the *nonskid* mats at the store entrances.

prefix:_____

root: _____

meaning of full word: _____

Answers to Skills Practice Exercise A are on page 304.

Exercise B

Read the following sentences. On the blank line following each sentence, write what the word in italics means based on your knowledge of the prefix and the root.

1. The loud noise outside *detracted* my attention from work.

_____

2. With its grand old building, the store was able to *preserve* a feeling of an earlier time.

_____

3. The customer is angry because the sales clerk *miscalculated* the bill.

_____

4. The *nondescript* person turned out to be a shop lifter.

_____

5. This complaint is *nonsense*.

_____

Check Yourself

Work Problem

You are receiving your yearly performance evaluation from Elena Del Santos. You must study her comments. They will show how you are doing and how you can improve.

PERFORMANCE EVALUATION FORM

EMPLOYEE: _____ (Your name) _____

DATE: _____ April 25, 199- _____

	ABOVE AVERAGE	AVERAGE	BELOW AVERAGE
Knowledge of Job	X		
Attitude	X		
Defers to Authority	X		
Attendance		X	

COMMENTS:

This person is an excellent employee, with high ability to deal with details. When faced with a problem, this individual can deduce a solution from the various facts. The individual smooths over misunderstandings with coworkers and does not take sides in office disagreements. I have no misgivings about recommending this employee for a position of increased authority.

Exercise

As you read, try to determine the meaning of any difficult words you find from your knowledge of prefixes.

1. nonaligned

       a) not taking sides
       b) paid by the hour
       c) uninsured
       d) underpaid

2. deduce

   a) figure out
   b) made smaller
   c) send
   d) place

3. defers

   a) disobeys
   b) understands
   c) accepts from another
   d) fails to obey orders

4. misgiving

   a) selfish
   b) meaning
   c) not generous
   d) doubt

5. misapplied

   a) mistaken meaning
   b) failed to listen
   c) refused to look
   d) used wrongly

Now consider your work problem and the form you are reading. Answer the following questions. Remember to define, plan, read, and check.

How can this form help you solve your work problem?

_____

_____

What conclusion can you draw about your work performance?

_____

_____

What should you do if you want to see if your performance has improved since your last evaluation?

_____

_____

Answers to Problem-Solving Practice Questions

Define Your Problem

What is my purpose for reading this material?

Decide whether message should be given to Monroe.

What should I be able to do when I finish reading?

Know whether message important to store operations.

Plan Your Solution

What information do I need from this material to solve my work problem?

Whether message applies to store operations.

How carefully will I have to read to find the information I need?

Skim entire message to find out if Mr. Monroe should see it.

Read

What information do the format clues give me?

Who message is for. Who it is from. Whether it requires a response.

What do I already know about this situation that will help me?

If message applies to store operations, I must pass it on to Mr. Monroe.

Should I continue reading this material?

Yes. Does Mr. Monroe need this information?

What information is important because it helps me solve my work problem?

Delivery is being held up. This could affect store operations.

Have I put the new and old information together and decided what to do?

Yes. Mr. Monroe must know what is happening (old). Shipment delayed (new).

| Check Your Solution |

Did I accomplish my purpose? (Did I draw a conclusion and make a decision?)

Yes. I found out that Mr. Monroe needs to be given the message.

Did the information help me solve my work problem? How?

Yes. Gave message to Mr. Monroe.

Answers to Skills Practice Exercise A

1. prefix: *de-*
   root: *crease*
   meaning of full word: "down, loss"
2. prefix: *mis-*
   root: *inform*
   meaning of full word: "wrong information (data)"
3. prefix: *non-*
   root: *abrasive*
   meaning of full word: "not abrasive, not rough or scratchy"
4. prefix: *de-*
   root: *tect*
   meaning of full word: "find out"
5. prefix: *non-*
   root: *skid*
   meaning of full word: "not slippery"

LESSON 15

Reading Tables
and Charts to Draw Conclusions

Many business documents use tables, charts, and other graphic materials to present information. Like all information, graphic information can help you draw a conclusion or make a decision about a work problem.

Look at the work schedule below for four employees at Enterprise Department Store. It is made up for one work week.

Enterprise Department Store STOCK CLERK SCHEDULE Week of March 6-12, 199–								
Stock Clerk		SUN	MON	TUE	WED	THU	FRI	SAT
Aborn, Danielle	IN	8AM		10AM		10AM		8AM
	OUT	3PM		4PM		4PM		3PM
Bennett, Theo	IN	3PM	3PM		3PM	3PM	3PM	3PM
	OUT	9PM	9PM		9PM	9PM	9PM	9PM
Ferace, Jordan	IN		8AM	8AM	8AM			
	OUT		2PM	4PM	3PM			
Franks, Chris	IN	8AM						3PM
	OUT	3PM						9PM

Title: What the document is about

Labels: Headings above **columns** tell what the information means

Form: A table

Labels: Headings along **rows** tell what the information means

Information: The table is arranged to make it easy to find information

Reading to Draw Conclusions

Now look at the Enterprise Department Store's time sheet again. See how Ernie Cesar reads it to draw a conclusion.

Enterprise will be having a big spring sale. Ernie has to be sure that two stock clerks are working from 8 A.M. to 9 P.M. Saturday and Sunday during the sale. He must look at the time chart and decide if the schedule should be revised.

1. He looks for information from the format clues. (This week's schedule; lists names, days, and times stock clerks work.)

Enterprise Department Store
STOCK CLERK SCHEDULE
Week of March 6–12, 199–

		SUN	MON	TUE	WED	THU	FRI	SAT
Aborn, Danielle	IN	8AM		10AM		10AM		8AM
	OUT	3PM		4PM		4PM		3PM
Bennett, Theo	IN	3PM	3PM		3PM	3PM	3PM	3PM
	OUT	9PM	9PM		9PM	9PM	9PM	9PM
Ferace, Jordan	IN		8AM	8AM	8AM			
	OUT		2PM	4PM	3PM			
Franks, Chris	IN	8AM						3PM
	OUT	3PM						9PM

2. He looks for what he already knows about the situation that will help him. (Time sheet shows hours employees work. Need at least two clerks to work 8 A.M. to 9 P.M. Saturday and Sunday.)

3. He decides whether to continue reading this material. (Yes, to find clerk to work Saturday 8 A.M. to 3 P.M. and Sunday 3 P.M. to 9 P.M.)

4. He picks out the information that helps him solve his work problem. (One clerk does not work on either Saturday or Sunday.)

5. He puts the new and the old information together to draw a conclusion. (This clerk might be the extra hand needed during sale. He decides to ask Jordon Ferace to work.)

You have seen how Ernie Cesar solved his work problem. Now work through another problem using the problem-solving strategy.

Work Problem

Gordon Jung is safety officer for Enterprise Department Stores. He makes a list of new safety equipment to order:

- Gloves for use in loading area—must provide secure grip so workers don't drop heavy cartons
- Gloves for cleaning staff—must protect hands against cleaning chemicals
- Step stool—must roll easily with rubber locking feet to adhere to floor

Gordon gives you the Commercial Safety Catalog to see if you can find the gloves in it. If you can, he wants you to give him the item numbers.

Commercial Safety Catalog		Table of Safety Gloves		
Item No.	Description	Unit Price	Per Dozen	
BT-9034-X	**Welders Glove** Leather. Protects against heat. Made of antishrink material. Long cuff.	14.95	169.00	
BT-4089-X	**Heavy Duty Latex Glove** Description: Ideal for commercial housekeeping. Resists all general-use cleaning chemicals. Comfortable lining, nonslip grip.	4.95	49.74	
BT-9001-X	**Heat-Resistant Glove** Description: Designed especially for conditions where temperatures are in excess of 250 degrees. Comes with custom made liner mitt.	24.75	256.00	
BT-7774-X	**Grip Supreme Super Strong Glove** Description: For heavy duty lifting, pulling, grabbing. Will not tear under continual use. Adjustable fasteners insure fit. Lined for warmth in outdoor use.	4.95	49.75	

Define Your Problem

What is my purpose for reading this material?

To decide if gloves on list are in catalog.

What should I be able to do when I finish reading?

Give Mr. Jung item numbers or say gloves unavailable.

Plan Your Solution

What information do I need from this material to solve my work problem?

Item numbers for gloves with secure grip for heavy use and for gloves that protect against cleaning chemicals.

How carefully will I have to read to find the information I need?

Carefully, to be sure the gloves I select are right for the jobs.

Read

What information do the format clues give me?

The table lists safety gloves with item numbers, description, and price.

What do I already know about this situation that will help me?

Two kinds of gloves are needed.

Should I continue reading this material?

Yes, to find item number for gloves I want.

What information is important because it helps me solve my work problem?

Description of the gloves.

Have I put the new and old information together and decided what to do?

Yes. They have the gloves we need, and item numbers are available.

| Check Your Solution |

Did I accomplish my purpose? (Did I draw a conclusion and make a decision?)

Yes. I found gloves to fit our needs.

Did the information help me solve my work problem? How?

Yes. I gave item numbers to Mr. Jung.

Problem-Solving Practice

Now apply your problem-solving strategy to another work problem.

Work Problem

Part of your job is to schedule repairs of appliances purchased at Enterprise. Joe Long handles all repairs that are under warranty (W). Martha Shore does repairs covered by a maintenance agreement (Ma). Herb Grandy handles repairs not covered by a warranty or a maintenance agreement.

Mr. Rao has called to say that his freezer needs adjusting. He purchased it six weeks ago. You refer to the Warranty/Maintenance Table below to decide which repair person will answer the call.

Warranty/Maintenance Table				
COVERAGE	90 DAYS	1ST YEAR	2ND YEAR	3RD YEAR
Replacement of Defective Parts	W	W	MA	MA
Mechanical Adjustments	W	MA	MA	MA
Porcelain and Glass Parts	MA	MA	MA	
Annual Preventive Maintenance	MA	MA	MA	

Define Your Problem

What is my purpose for reading this material?

_____

_____

What should I be able to do when I finish reading?

_____

_____

_____

_____

Plan Your Solution

What information do I need from this
material to solve my work problem?

_____

_____

_____

_____

How carefully will I have to read to find
the information I need?

_____

_____

_____

Read

What information do the format clues
give me?

_____

_____

_____

_____

What do I already know about this
situation that will help me?

_____

_____

_____

_____

Should I continue reading this material?

_____

_____

_____

_____

What information is important because
it helps me solve my work problem?

_____

_____

_____

_____

Have I put the new and old information
together and decided what to do?

_____

_____

_____

Check Your Solution

Did I accomplish my purpose? (Did I draw
a conclusion and make a decision?)

_____

_____

_____

_____

Did the information help me solve my
work problem? How?

_____

_____

_____

_____

Answers to the Problem-Solving Practice questions are on pages 322-324.

On Your Own

Now you will read four more tables and charts to draw conclusions. Remember to define your problem and plan your solution. Read and, if you need to, reread some or all of the material carefully. Finally, check to see if you have solved your problem.

Work Problem A

Customers often call with problems that do not require an appliance repair service call. You must help the customer fix the problem, if possible, before scheduling a service call.

Today, a customer called because his clothes dryer would not start. You refer to the Troubleshooting Chart below. You ask the customer to check each step to see if you must send a service repair person.

			TROUBLESHOOTING CHART
			Check these points before sending service person.
WON'T START	WON'T HEAT	DOESN'T DRY CLOTHES SATISFACTORILY	POSSIBLE REASON— DO THIS TO CORRECT
•			Be sure the cord is plugged all the way into electrical outlet.
•	•		Replace fuse. Reset circuit breaker. A 240-volt dryer has two fuses. Make sure both are good and also tight.
•			Close door.
	•		Make sure Dryness Control is at a Heat setting.
•			Push Start Control or move lever to Start.
	•		If you have a gas dryer, check to see if gas valve in dryer (behind front access panel) and main gas line valve are turned on.
		•	Adjust Automatic Cycle (if your dryer has one) to more or less dry setting.
		•	Timed Cycle—Allow more time.
		•	Clean lint screen.
		•	Check exhaust duct to outside to see if it is kinked, blocked, or needs cleaning.

How can this chart help you solve your work problem?

_____

_____

In which column on the chart will you find the problem described? In which column will you find the possible reason and a solution?

_____

_____

If the cord is plugged all the way into the outlet, and the dryer still does not work, what do you tell the customer to do?

_____

_____

What will you decide if the customer follows your directions and the dryer will still not start?

_____

_____

Work Problem B

Taking inventory at Enterprise is important. The first step is counting each item in the store. As each step is completed, information moves to the next person or people in the process. The team leader gets the final information. Lena Rose asks you to review an inventory process chart she prepared and tell her if it is correct.

Enterprise Department Store
INVENTORY PROCESS CHART

TEAM LEADER
Responsible for overseeing entire inventory taking.

CALLER/WRITER TEAM
Counts & lists merchandise on inventory sheet

AUDITORS
Spot check inventory sheets to be sure information is listed correctly. Make sure workers are not inconsistent.

SHEET COLLECTORS
Collect inventory sheets & return them to team leader.

How can this chart help you solve your work problem?

_____

_____

How is this chart organized?

_____

_____

Which group starts the inventory process? Where are they shown?

_____

_____

What is the correct order of the steps in the inventory process?

_____

_____

Work Problem C

You work for Nancy Macky in the hat department at Enterprise. You are reviewing the inventory chart for the department. Nancy asks you to note whether last season's hats were good sellers. You know that
- merchandise marked Y under Season Code is left from the season before
- merchandise marked R under Season Code is this season's inventory
- if there are more than twenty units of an item from last season in inventory, the item did not sell well

Enterprise Department Store HATS DEPARTMENT INVENTORY SHEET		
Mdse. No.	Season Code	No. of Units In Inventory
204	Y	7
214	R	45
222	R	12
223	Y	2
238	Y	28
239	Y	21
242	R	60
253	Y	6

How can this chart help you solve your work problem?

_____

_____

What are the merchandise numbers for hats from last season?

_____

_____

What are the merchandise numbers for last season's hats that have less than twenty units still in inventory? Did these items sell well or poorly?

_____

_____

What are the merchandise numbers for last season's hats that have more than twenty units still in inventory? Did these items sell well or poorly?

_____

_____

Work Problem D

Lena Rose needs a new printer for her office. The computer store she contacted gave her a chart. The chart lists four different printers that are compatible (work with) with her computer. She asks you to review the chart and recommend the printer to buy. She wants a printer that
  • prints quickly
  • can handle printouts of inventory sheets that measure 11 x 17 inches
  • costs less than $2,000

She does not care how many fonts it has.

CHART COMPARING PRINTERS				
MODEL	PRICE	SPEED ppm*	MAXIMUM PAPER SIZE	FONTS
Elite	$1999	6 ppm	11x17	3
BestAll	$1395	5 ppm	8.5x14	7
ClearPrint	$2295	8 ppm	8.5x14	5
LaserPrint	$3995	6 ppm	8.5x14	8
*ppm = pages per minute				

How can this chart help you solve your work problem?

_____

_____

What new and old information must you combine to draw a conclusion?

_____

_____

What information does the chart give you to help you draw a conclusion?

_____

_____

What printer might you tell Lena Rose to buy?

_____

_____

Skills Practice: Finding a Word's Meaning

Deciding a word's meaning by breaking it into parts often works well. Remember to make sure the meaning of the word makes sense in the sentence it is in.

You must always be careful. Some prefixes can have different meanings in different contexts. Suffixes can also give words different meanings.

Here is an example of a prefix that has two meanings:

Prefix	**(Meaning)**
in-	(in, into, or within)
in-	(not)

Example: Earlier, you read about *inventory*. *Inventory* starts with the prefix *in-* meaning "in," "into," or "within."

Inventory means "a list of items in stock."

Example: You also read this sentence:

   Make sure workers are not *inconsistent*.

The word *inconsistent* also begins with *in-*. *Consistent* means "being the same." This time *in-* means "not." *Inconsistent* means "not the same."

Now consider how a suffix can change a word's meaning.

Example: Earlier, you read this phrase:

   Annual *Preventive* Maintenance

You have already met the prefix *pre-* meaning "before." The root *ven* means "come."

Prevent, an action word, means "to stop, to keep from happening."

But the phrase "Annual Preventive Maintenance" does not mean to stop maintenance. The action word *prevent* is changed by the suffix *-tive*.

Prevent becomes *preventive*. *Preventive* is not an action word. It is now a word that describes something that stops or keeps from happening.

   Preventive maintenance "stops" (prevents) problems.

Here are two more useful prefixes to know:

Prefix **(Meaning)**

anti- (against)

Example: Earlier, you read this:

Made of *antishrink* material

Shrink means "to become smaller." *Antishrink* material is material that will not become smaller.

Prefix **(Meaning)**

ad- (toward, at)

Example: Earlier you read this.

Rubber locking feet to *adhere* to floor.

The root *here* means "to stick." *Adhere* means "to stick to or grasp."

Exercise A

Identify the prefix of the word in italics. Write the prefix, suffix, if any, and the root in the space provided. Give the meaning of the prefix and the full word.

1. There is a parking lot *adjacent* to the store.

   prefix:＿＿＿＿＿ meaning: ＿＿＿＿＿＿＿＿＿＿＿＿＿＿＿＿＿＿＿

   suffix: ＿＿＿＿＿＿＿＿＿＿＿＿＿＿＿＿＿＿＿＿＿＿＿＿＿＿＿＿＿

   root: ＿＿＿＿＿＿＿＿＿＿＿＿＿＿＿＿＿＿＿＿＿＿＿＿＿＿＿＿＿＿＿

   meaning of full word: ＿＿＿＿＿＿＿＿＿＿＿＿＿＿＿＿＿＿＿＿＿＿

2. The company medical plan supports *preventive* medicine.

   prefix:＿＿＿＿＿ meaning: ＿＿＿＿＿＿＿＿＿＿＿＿＿＿＿＿＿＿＿

   suffix: ＿＿＿＿＿＿＿＿＿＿＿＿＿＿＿＿＿＿＿＿＿＿＿＿＿＿＿＿＿

   root: ＿＿＿＿＿＿＿＿＿＿＿＿＿＿＿＿＿＿＿＿＿＿＿＿＿＿＿＿＿＿＿

   meaning of full word: ＿＿＿＿＿＿＿＿＿＿＿＿＿＿＿＿＿＿＿＿＿＿

3. He understood the problem and made *insightful* suggestions for solving it.

   prefix:＿＿＿＿＿ meaning: ＿＿＿＿＿＿＿＿＿＿＿＿＿＿＿＿＿＿＿

   suffix: ＿＿＿＿＿＿＿＿＿＿＿＿＿＿＿＿＿＿＿＿＿＿＿＿＿＿＿＿＿

   root: ＿＿＿＿＿＿＿＿＿＿＿＿＿＿＿＿＿＿＿＿＿＿＿＿＿＿＿＿＿＿＿

   meaning of full word: ＿＿＿＿＿＿＿＿＿＿＿＿＿＿＿＿＿＿＿＿＿＿

4. The appliance is built of *antirust* material.

   prefix:_____   meaning: _____

   suffix:_____

   root: _____

   meaning of full word: _____

5. Our supervisor encourages *adherence* to the policy.

   prefix:_____   meaning: _____

   suffix:_____

   root: _____

   meaning of full word: _____

Answers to Skills Practice Exercise A are on page 324.

Exercise B

In each sentence below, identify the prefix of the word in italics. Write the prefix and its meaning in the space provided. Then write the meaning of the full word.

1. We are going to *preview* the new season's line of clothing.

   prefix:_____   meaning: _____

   meaning of full word: _____

2. They do not have all the facts, so they have drawn an *invalid* conclusion.

   prefix:_____   meaning: _____

   meaning of full word: _____

3. We carry a line of clothing for *preschool* children.

   prefix:_____   meaning: _____

   meaning of full word: _____

4. This glue has poor *adhesion*, so all the charts fell off the wall.

   prefix:_____   meaning: _____

   meaning of full word: _____

5. Because nobody believes him, he is *ineffectual* as a group leader.

   prefix:_____   meaning: _____

   meaning of full word: _____

Check Yourself

Work Problem

Elena Del Santos is sending a letter to customers. The letter offers customers a special sale. She wants the letter to go to those who
- have spent more than $500 at the department store in the past year
- do not have overdue balances

She has made a list of customers to receive the offer. The billing department gave you a list of all customers who have purchased items during the past twelve months. Now she asks you to check her list.

Customer Purchases Prior 12-Month Period			
Customer	**Card #**	**Purchase Amt**	**Amt of Arrears**
Caruso, Steve	33487	$1,300.00	$300
Clancy, Amy	33561	$640.00	0
Cronin, Tina	33158	$300.00	0
Ellis, Juan	32678	$100.00	0
Janeiro, Luis	32509	$750.00	0
Petrowsky, Mel	32073	$800.00	$500

How can this list help you solve your work problem?

_____

_____

What columns on the list are important for you to read?

_____

_____

Do any of the customers listed still owe the store money?

_____

_____

What names would you take off the list you are checking? Why?

_____

_____

Exercise

Consider the numbered words below. Circle the word in the list that you feel means most nearly the same as each numbered word.

1. Arrears (See Customer Purchase List)

   a) debt
   b) past
   c) before
   d) behind

2. Overseeing (See Inventory Process Chart)

   a) looking
   b) not seeing
   c) missing
   d) managing

3. Defective (See Warranty/Maintenance Table)

   a) lost
   b) unused
   c) late
   d) unusable

Answers to Problem-Solving Practice Questions

Define Your Problem

What is my purpose for reading this material?

To decide who should handle repair.

What should I be able to do when I finish reading?

Assign repair work if necessary.

Plan Your Solution

What information do I need from this material to solve my work problem?

Is repair under warranty, maintenance, or neither?

How carefully will I have to read to find the information I need?

Step by step. If I make wrong decision, I will send wrong person to make repair.

Read

What information do the format clues give me?

Amount of time repairs are covered by warranty and by maintenance.

What do I already know about this situation that will help me?

I know which repair person handles which kind of repair.

Should I continue reading this material?

No. I'm ready to compare info and make decision.

What information is important because it helps me solve my work problem?

Mr. Rao purchased the freezer six weeks ago— within 90 days.

Have I put the new and old information together and decided what to do?

Yes. I see the repair is under warranty. I know whom to assign it to.

Check Your Solution

Did I accomplish my purpose? (Did I draw a conclusion and make a decision?)

Yes. I assigned repair to Joe Long.

Did the information help me solve my work problem? How?

Yes. I decided who should handle repair.

Answers to Skills Practice Exercise A

1. prefix: *ad-* meaning: "toward, at"
   suffix: none
   root: *jacent*
   meaning of full word: "next to"
2. prefix: *pre-* meaning "before"
   suffix: *-tive*
   root: *vent*
   meaning of full word: "prevents (stops) problems"
3. prefix: *in-* means "in"
   suffix: *-ful*
   root: *sight*
   meaning of full word: "see into, understand"
4. prefix: *anti-* means "against"
   suffix: none
   root: *rust*
   meaning of full word: "will not rust"
5. prefix: *ad-* means "to"
   suffix: *-ence*
   root: *courage*
   meaning of full word: "staying with, sticking to"

LESSON 16

Reading Reference Books to Draw Conclusions

Reference books are good sources for many kinds of information. When you need to make an important decision, you will often consult reference books. Catalogs or guides listing businesses are common references people in business use. Here is a sample page from a guide listing companies that sell building supplies.

This Year's Home Center Operators Guide   p. 12

Cape Home Centers
70 Columbia Highway, Camden, NJ 08100

Telephone: 609-111-1111

Product Lines: BBQ Equipment, Cabinets, Carpeting, Ceiling/Skylights, Fireplace Equipment, Housewares, Kitchen/Bath Accessories, Lawn & Garden Supplies, Lighting Fixtures, Power Equipment and Tools, Roofing, Windows & Doors

Annual Sales: $4,000,000
# of Stores: 5
Offers Delivery: Yes (5 trucks)
Year Founded: 1957

Reading to Draw Conclusions

Ellie Rodin is sales manager at Major Manufacturing. Major has sold power tools to Cape Home Centers for years. Recently Cape orders have fallen. Ms. Rodin reads the information on Cape Home Centers in this year's and last year's issues of the Home Center Operator's Guide. Here is how Ms. Rodin read them to draw conclusions.

1. She looks for information from the format clues. (Information given in categories)

2. She looks for what she already knows about the situation that will help her. (Sales of Major products to Cape have declined.)

Last Year's Home Center Operators Guide   p. 10

Cape Home Centers
70 Columbia Highway, Camden, NJ 08100

Telephone: 609-111-1111

Product Lines: Cabinets, Carpeting, Ceiling/Skylights, Fireplace Equipment, Housewares, Kitchen/Bath Accessories, Lawn & Garden Supplies, Power Equipment and Tools

Annual Sales: $3,500,000
# of Stores: 4
Offers Delivery: Yes (5 trucks)
Year Founded: 1957

---

3. She decides whether to continue reading this material. (Yes. She wants to find whether something has changed at Cape.)

4. She picks out the information that helps her solve her work problem. (Product line, number of stores, and annual sales.)

5. She puts the new and the old information together to draw a conclusion. (She sees that Cape is doing well. She decides that Major should promote their products more aggressively to Cape to increase Major sales.)

Ms Rodin used the problem-solving strategy to draw conclusions from the directory. Let's go through another problem using this strategy.

Work Problem

You are assistant to the head of personnel at Major. is preparing a speech to honor employees who have been with the company twenty-five years. He gives you his first draft. He wants to you make changes anywhere he might have used biased language. You compare the speech with the page in the company manual on bias-free writing below:

Major Manufacturing Company Policy Manual   p.16

BIAS-FREE LANGUAGE

It is company policy to avoid insensitive language in all company publications and correspondence. Persons speaking in the company's name are urged to follow these guidelines also.

Refer to men and women in the same style.

USE	DO NOT USE
Bill Graves and Anita Jones	Bill Graves and Mrs. Jones
or	or
Mr. Graves and Ms. Jones	Mr. Graves and Anita Jones

Use the same title for both men and women in the same job or position.

USE	DO NOT USE
Sam Ho, chairperson of committee A	Sam Ho, chairman of committee A
and	and
Beth Bojak, chairperson of committee B	Beth Bojak, chairwoman of committee B.

Avoid terms that suggest only men or only women when both men and women are involved. Use *work force* rather than *manpower*. Use *close associate* rather than *right-hand man*.

Always avoid objectionable or offensive names such as *girl* or *boy* when referring to adults.

Welcome Ladies and Gentlemen:

You are here to be honored by the company for your twenty-five years of service to Major Manufacturing Company. Each and every one of you has made an important contribution, whether it is finding a better way to serve our clients, acting as chairman of a committee, or being a loyal and hardworking contributor to manpower at Major. One of you, Nick Colt, joined Major right after school. Another, Mrs. Rho, joined Major after a number of years as a teacher. You all have interesting stories to tell about your experiences here at Major Manufacturing Company. We are proud of your deeds.

Define Your Problem

What is my purpose for reading this material?

To decide whether speech uses biased language.

What should I be able to do when I finish reading?

Take out biased language.

Plan Your Solution

What information do I need from this material to solve my work problem?

Examples of biased and bias-free writing in manual.

How carefully will I have to read to find the information I need?

Carefully, to compare examples of biased language in manual to speech.

Read

What information do the format clues give me?

One page is from the company manual and the other is from the speech.

What do I already know about this situation that will help me?

Writer is concerned about using biased language, which may offend people.

Should I continue reading this material?

Yes, to see whether manual will help identify biased words.

What information is important because it helps me solve my work problem?

Biased terms in the speech and information from the manual.

Have I put the new and old information together and decided what to do?

Yes. I found examples of biased language.

Check Your Solution

Did I accomplish my purpose? (Did I draw a conclusion and make a decision?)

Yes. I changed biased language to unbiased language.

Did the information help me solve my work problem? How?

Yes. I identified and changed biased language.

Problem-Solving Practice

Now apply your strategy to another work problem.

Work Problem

Your company's computer printer is not working. It is a Star Model 900. The store you bought it from has moved out of town. You could call the original store, but you prefer to find a local store to fix it.

A local store would be more likely to send someone to your office. Also, having a local repair service would be good in case of future problems. You look in the yellow pages and try to find a company.

Barney's Best Computers and Printers!

Wide selection of large and small computers and print-ers—over 15 different makes. Over 2000 satisfied cus-tomers last year makes us the fastest growing computer store in the region.

Our experienced sales staff is eager to help you make the right choice for your office needs.

Special evening hours Thursdays and Saturdays—open til 9 P.M. Free coffee or glass of wine while you shop.

Open Sundays til 5 P.M.
Service contracts on all new equipment.
Visit our office at Coleman and Broad.

222-5555

L & A Office & Home Equipment
120 Main Street   **321-5433**
Authorized dealer of Star Printers

- We sell new & used equipment
- We've been serving the business community for 25 years

Bring in your equipment or call to have one of our skilled technicians come to your office.

Define Your Problem

What is my purpose for reading this material?

_____

_____

What should I be able to do when I finish
reading?

_____

_____

| Plan Your Solution |

What information do I need from this
material to solve my work problem?

_____

_____

_____

_____

How carefully will I have to read to find
the information I need?

_____

_____

_____

| Read |

What information do the format clues
give me?

_____

_____

_____

_____

What do I already know about this
situation that will help me?

_____

_____

_____

_____

Should I continue reading this material?

_____

_____

What information is important because
it helps me solve my work problem?

_____

_____

_____

_____

Have I put the new and old information
together and decided what to do?

_____

_____

_____

| Check Your Solution |

Did I accomplish my purpose? (Did I
draw a conclusion and make a decision?)

_____

_____

_____

_____

Did the information help me solve my
work problem? How?

_____

_____

_____

_____

Answers to the Problem-Solving Practice questions are on pages 342-344.

On Your Own

Now you will look at four more work problems in which you read reference books to draw conclusions. Remember to define your purpose and plan your solution. Read, and then, if you need to, reread some or all of the pages carefully. Finally, check to see if you have solved your problem.

Work Problem A

You are the assistant to Ellie Rodin, marketing director at Major Manufacturing. Ms. Rodin wants to send a promotional letter to hardware chain store operators in Georgia. She wants to send the letter only to stores that have the following qualifications:

- Four or more stores in the chain
- A product line that includes power equipment
- Annual sales of at least $2 million

You look in the Directory of Hardware Store Owners.

Directory of Georgia Hardware Store Owners   p. 22

Galt Hardware
76 Adams St., Augusta, GA 30900
Telephone: 404-222-4441
Product Lines: BBQ Equipment, Cabinets, Ceiling/Skylights, Farm Supplies, Fireplace Equipment, Insulation, Kitchen/Bath Fixtures, Lawn & Garden Supplies, Lighting Fixtures, Lumber, Paints, Plumbing-Heating-Cooling Equipment, Power Equipment and Tools, Roofing, Windows & Doors, Distributor of Fine Homes Paints
Annual Sales: $1,250,000
# of Stores: 5
Owner: Sally Galt; **Buyer**: Jason Wells
Year Founded: 1957

Red Eagle Lumber and Hardware
54 Lanier St., Columbus, GA 31900
Telephone: 404-332-1441
Product Lines: Cabinets, Ceiling/Skylights, Insulation, Lighting Fixtures, Lumber, Paints, Plumbing-Heating-Cooling Equipment, Power Equipment and Tools, Roofing, Windows & Doors
Annual Sales: $2,250,000
# of Stores: 4
Owner and Buyer: Bill Tate
Year Founded: 1948

Titus-Mobay Hardware and Housewares
77 Cyprus Ave., Savannah, GA 31400
Telephone: 912-312-3441
Product Line: BBQ Equipment, Cabinets, Ceiling/Skylights, Fireplace Equipment, Insulation, Housewares, Kitchen/Bath Fixtures, Lawn & Garden Supplies, Lighting Fixtures, Paints, Wall Paper, Windows & Doors
Annual Sales: $6,000,000
# of Stores: 8
Owner: Terry Titus
Buyer: Westina Smith

How can this page help you solve your work problem?

_____

_____

Which of Ms. Rodin's qualifications does Galt Hardware have?

_____

_____

Which of Ms. Rodin's qualifications does Red Eagle Lumber and Hardware have?

_____

_____

Which company names do you give to Ms. Rodin?

_____

_____

Work Problem B

Ms. Rodin wants to set up a special display of new garden tools at one hardware store in the region. She asks you to choose one of three companies—Russo, Goldstein, or B & J. She wants a company that

- carries a lot of outdoor supplies and equipment
- has a large number of branch stores

Directory of Illinois Hardware Store Owners   p. 42

B & J Hardware
16 Roger St., Belleville, IL 62220
Telephone: 618-277-7777
Product Lines: BBQ Equipment, Cabinets, Ceiling/Skylights, Fireplace Equipment, Insulation, Lighting Fixtures, Lumber, Paints, Plumbing-Heating-Cooling Equipment, Power Equipment, and Tools, Sinks and Tubs, Wallpaper
Annual Sales: $2,250,000
# of Stores: 5
Offers Delivery: Yes

Goldstein Hardware and Housewares
2702 Lakeside Ave., Belleville, IL 62220
Telephone: 618-458-3530
Product Lines: Product Line: Cabinets, Ceiling/Skylights, Fireplace Equipment, Housewares, Insulation, Kitchenware, Lighting Fixtures, Paints, Sinks and Tubs, Shower Curtains, Wallpaper, Window Shades
Annual Sales: $5,250,000
# of Stores: 7
Offers Delivery: Yes

Russo Hardware
66 Park St., Alton, IL 62002
Telephone: 618-830-9531
Product Line: Animal Feed, BBQ Equipment, Cabinets, Fireplace Equipment, Garden Tools and Supplies, Insulation, Lawn Care Equipment and Supplies, Lighting Fixtures, Lumber, Outdoor Furniture, Paints, Pet Supplies, Plumbing-Heating-Cooling Equipment, Power Equipment and Tools, Roofing, Sinks and Tubs, Wallpaper
Annual Sales: $2,500,000
# of Stores: 4
Offers Delivery: Yes

How can this page help you solve your work problem?

_____

_____

Which company carries the most outdoor supplies and equipment?

_____

_____

Which company has the most stores?

_____

_____

Which company do you recommmend to Ms. Rodin? Why?

_____

_____

Work Problem C

Each year Jerry Simpson does a market survey to get information for ad campaigns for the coming year. Last year Key Market Research Company conducted the survey. They did a good job, but Mr. Simpson would like to try another company this year. He tells you he wants a company with the following qualifications:

- Specializes in surveys of consumers
- Uses telephone surveys
- Has worked with regional retail businesses

You look in the Directory of Market Research and find three in your city.

Directory of Illinois Market Researchers

Sarah Arthur Associates
950 Route 43, Alton, IL 62002
Telephone: 618-888-8877

Specialists in market research including telephone and mail surveys and personal interviews.
Services can be provided for a complete project or for just a part.
Clients include Edenville Department Store, R & L Garden Products, and other retail businesses throughout the region.

Key Market Research
50 South Main, Alton, IL 62002
Telephone: 618-998-7799

We provide all phases of market research: study design, interviewing, and analysis. We use telephone surveys, mail, and personal interview techniques.
Our clients include national and international corporations.
We specialize in medical and technical fields.

Rico/Kaltis Research
48 Thompson Square, Alton, IL 62002
Telephone: 618-998-7799

For over fifteen years we have provided highly focused market research by means of telephone surveys and in-depth research and analysis techniques.
Clients include regional professional associations and institutions.
Our specialty is political campaign surveys.

38

How can this page help you solve your work problem?

_____

_____

Would you recommend Sarah Arthur Associates? Why?

_____

_____

Would you recommend going back to Key Market Research? Why?

_____

_____

Would you recommend Rico/Kaltis? Why?

_____

_____

Work Problem D

Phil Crosley asks you to read the draft of a letter he has written. It will be sent to a number of people, and he wants to be sure his wording is not insensitive. You look at your manual for bias-free writing and compare it to Phil's letter.

Dear Gentlemen:

We are pleased to introduce a new product that we are sure will be of interest to you and your fellow engineers. I have enclosed a flyer that describes it in detail.

Please take a few minutes from your busy schedule to read it.

One of our salesmen will be in your area soon and will call to discuss this product with you. Alert your secretary so she can help set up a meeting.

Share the flyer with a colleague. He will thank you for the information.

If you have questions, please do not hesitate to call me.

Sincerely,

Major Manufacturing Company Policy Manual   p.17
BIAS-FREE LANGUAGE

Treat men and women with the same repect. Avoid assumptions or stereotyped descriptions. For example, do not assume all doctors are men and all secretaries are women. When addressing a group of people

USE	DO NOT USE
colleagues coworkers men and women	fellow workers

Use titles and job descriptions that are not gender-specific.

USE	DO NOT USE
public relations specialist	public relations man

How can these materials help you solve your work problem?

_____

_____

List examples that show how Phil has not followed the company guidelines on bias-free writing.

_____

_____

How else might Phil say, "One of our salesmen"?

_____

_____

Can you suggest to Phil a better way to write the fourth paragraph? Write it below.

_____

_____

Skills Practice: Finding a Word's Meaning

You have learned many prefixes in earlier lessons. Here are two more that are useful.

Prefix   **(Meaning)**

ob-   (against or directed toward in a negative way)

Example: In the company manual on bias-free writing, you read this:

   Always avoid *objectionable* or offensive names.

Objectionable contains the prefix *ob-* and the root word *jection*. *Objectionable* means "causing offense or diapproval."

Prefix   **(Meaning)**

dis-   (away or apart)

Example: In the page from the Directory of Georgia Hardware Store Owners, you saw this phrase:

   Distributor of Fine Homes Paints

The word *distributor* starts with the prefix *dis-*. A *distributor* " delivers, passes out, spreads." In this case, the distributor sends the products away from the maker.

Exercise A

In each sentence below, identify the prefix of the word in italics. Write the prefix and its meaning in the space below the sentence. Then write the meaning of the full word.

1. We could not deliver the order because there was an *obstacle* in the road.

   prefix:_____   meaning: _____

   meaning of full word: _____

2. She cannot see the avenue from her office window because another building *obstructs* her view.

   prefix:_____   meaning: _____

   meaning of full word: _____

3. We are willing to *invest* our money in the new product.

   prefix:_____   meaning: _____

   meaning of full word: _____

4. The price of the coat *exceeds* what customers are willing to pay for it.

   prefix:_____   meaning: _____

   meaning of full word: _____

5. The prices have *declined* a lot, so now is a good time to buy.

prefix:_____   meaning: _____

meaning of full word: _____

Answers to Skills Practice Exercise A are on page 344.

Exercise B

In each sentence below, identify the prefix and the root of the word in italics. Write the prefix and root with their meanings in the space below the sentence. Then write the meaning for the full word.

1. The housewares company has a small *subsidiary* that sells only kitchenwares.

   Prefix: _____   meaning: _____

   Root:_____   meaning: _____

   meaning of full word: _____

2. He decided to *retain* the consultant for another two months because his advice had been so good.

   Prefix: _____   meaning: _____

   Root:_____   meaning: _____

   meaning of full word: _____

3. Upon *reflection*, we are not ready to sign the contract because we still have several questions.

   Prefix: _____   meaning: _____

   Root:_____   meaning: _____

   meaning of full word: _____

4. The meaning of their letter is *obscure*, and I cannot not figure out what they want us to do.

   Prefix: _____   meaning: _____

   Root:_____   meaning: _____

   meaning of full word: _____

5. The two new workers are doing a very good job. They *excel* in all their tasks.

   Prefix: _____   meaning: _____

   Root:_____   meaning: _____

   meaning of full word: _____

Check Yourself

Work Problem

C.C. Ma is the product development manager at Major Manufacturing. He has just returned from the Annual Plastics Expo. While there, he saw the exhibit of Taylor Plastics. He was impressed with their product, and he thinks that Major should do business with Taylor. They might manufacture plastic handles for Major tools.

He asks you to look up Taylor in the Plastics Industry Directory. He would like to know

- How long the company has been in business
- What they produce
- Where they are located
- Where they sell their products

You find Taylor in the directory.

Plastics Industry Directory   page 33

Taylor Plastics is based in Chesterton, IL. For twenty-five years it has been designing and manufacturing plastic containers at four plants in the Midwest. It is the dominant maker of shampoo bottles, but its sales pattern is changeable for other containers.

Recently **Taylor** opened a new engineering and manufacturing complex in Ross River that employs 230 people. At this site, **Taylor** is developing and manufacturing heavy-duty products. These include tool handles and car parts.

The company has worldwide distribution. Sales were $200 million last year, about a third of which came from exports.

Taylor is regarded as a well-run business with competent managers who are knowledgeable and skilled.

Exercise

Before solving the work problem, try to determine the meaning of the words below from your knowledge of prefixes and roots and from the context in which you find the words.

1. dominant

    a) leading
    b) worst
    c) foreign
    d) incomplete

2. complex

    a) container
    b) tool
    c) plant
    d) product

3. distribution

   a) donation
   b) sales and marketing
   c) problems
   d) information

4. exports

   a) heavy-duty tools
   b) products sold in this country
   c) products sold outside this country
   d) products that do not sell

5. competent

   a) kind
   b) biased
   c) bias-free
   d) capable

Now consider your work problem and the information you are reading. Answer the following questions. Remember to define, plan, read, and check.

How can this directory page help you solve your work problem?

_____

_____

What can you tell Mr. Ma about how long Taylor has been in business?

_____

_____

What can you tell Mr. Ma about what Taylor produces and where Taylor sells its products?

_____

_____

What can you tell Mr. Ma about tools handles made at Taylor?

_____

_____

Answers to Problem-Solving Practice Questions

Define Your Problem

What is my purpose for reading this material?

To find a local company to repair my computer.

What should I be able to do when I finish reading?

Pick one of two companies to call for repairs.

Plan Your Solution

What information do I need from this material to solve my work problem?

A company that does repairs, will come to my office, and knows Star printers.

How carefully will I have to read to find the information I need?

Carefully. Both ads may have useful information.

Read

What information do the format clues give me?

This is section on office equipment from the yellow pages.

What do I already know about this situation that will help me?

Yellow pages will list most stores in area. I'm familiar with printer and can judge who could help.

Should I continue reading this material?

I must find out if either or both companies do repairs.

What information is important because it helps me solve my work problem?

Who repairs Star printers and can they send someone to do the repair?

Have I put the new and old information together and decided what to do?

Yes. L & A can provide service, is Star dealer, and can send someone to office.

Check Your Solution

Did I accomplish my purpose? (Did I draw a conclusion and make a decision?)

Yes. I called L & A.

Did the information help me solve my work problem? How?

Yes. I found local company to repair printer.

Answers to Skills Practice Exercise A

1. Prefix: *ob-* means "away or apart"
   Meaning of full word: "bar, barrier"
2. Prefix: *ob-* means "away or apart"
   Meaning of full word: block, bar
3. Prefix: *in-* means "within"
   Meaning of full word: "put into, instill"
4. Prefix: *ex-* means "out"
   Meaning of full word: "goes beyond, goes above"
5. Prefix: *de-* means "down, from"
   Meaning of full word: "went down"

Putting It All Together

You are again on the job as an intern at MailMart. Remember that this large firm sells clothing and sporting goods throughout the country. It sells mostly through catalogs. It also runs a large store that people visit from all over. As an intern learning the business, you are required to work in many different jobs.

Work Problem A

You have been assigned to the accounting department of MailMart. Fred Montoya is in charge of this department. He is the company controller.

He says, "You should be aware of our accounting policies. If you are going to be a bookkeeper, you should know why an accounting system is necessary." He suggests that you read the information in the company policy manual.

Look at the documents on the following pages. Read the one that will help you solve your problem. Then answer the following questions.

Which document did you select to read?

_____

_____

How can this document help you solve your work problem?

_____

_____

What are some of the reasons MailMart keeps records?

_____

_____

What is the purpose of having internal controls in a record keeping system?

_____

_____

What are the parts of a record-keeping system?

_____

_____

Work Problem B

Israel Rojas called a meeting of all employees to talk about a possible problem at the company. He talks about the need for all workers to get along with each other. He ends by saying, "We must all work together. Only in that way can the company continue to succeed. And the company's success is your success."

He then distributes a sheet of paper. He says, "These are new policies that will be put in the company manual. Everyone please read them."

Look at the documents on the following pages. Read the one that will help you solve your problem. Then answer the following questions.

Which document did you select to read?

_____

_____

How can this document help you solve your work problem?

_____

_____

What are the five sections in the new policies?

_____

_____

What does it mean to patronize others? Why would it upset someone to be patronized?

_____

_____

DATE: March 4, 199—

FROM: Israel Rojas, General Manager

TO: All Department Managers

SUBJECT: FALL CATALOG MEETING

This is to notify all department managers of the Fall Catalog Meeting. This is an important meeting to prepare the fall catalog. All managers must attend.

The meeting will be held March 18 beginning at 8:30 a.m. in the conference room. The meeting, as usual, will last all day. Please be sure to mark your calendars.

In addition to the usual items, we will discuss the following new items and prices to be included in the fall catalog. If we all agree, these will go in the catalog.

Item	Price
Crewneck Ragg Sweaters	
Men's Regular Dyed	$29.50
Men's Regular Gray	$25.50
Women's Dyed	$29.50
Women's Gray	$25.50
Shawl Collar Ragg Sweaters	
Men's Regular Dyed	$35.00
Men's Regular Gray	$32.00
Women's Dyed	$35.00
Women's Gray	$32.00
Plaid Shirts	
Men's Regular	$21.50
Men's Tall	$23.00
Women's	$21.00
Stretch Denim Jeans	
Men's	$35.00
Women's	$35.00

Thank you and see you at the meeting.

MAILMART COMPANY POLICY MANUAL

Part 3—Policies for Telephone: Handling Complaint Calls

Whenever you are handling a complaint call, here is a list of what you should remember to do:

1. Slow your rate of speech.

2. Lower volume of your voice.

3. Express regret for any misunderstanding. Try to find a point of agreement.

4. Tell the caller that you will be jotting down the details as they speak to help you resolve the situation.

5. Ask intelligent questions. Listen attentively to the answers. Take good notes.

6. Read back what you have written. Use a lead-in phrase such as: "To make certain I understand, let's review what we've gone over . . ."

7. Tell the person making the complaint what steps you will take to correct the situation.

8. Make a promise to correct the situation THAT CAN BE KEPT.

9. Fulfill the promise.

10. Make a follow-up call to check the customer's satisfaction.

MAILMART COMPANY POLICY MANUAL

<u>Part 4—Policies for Maintaining Records</u>

The Importance of Keeping Rcords

A good set of books provides us with a data base, a road map. Up-to-date and correct records tell us where we have been and where we are, so that managers can make sound decisions. A complete bookkeeping system furnishes the figures we need to prepare tax forms. The system also alerts our managers to problems.

Sound data helps managers find realistic answers to such questions as:

1. Did we make any profit last month? If so, how much?

2. Where is the money going?

3. Which customers warrant the most attention, good or bad? Who should be encouraged to buy more? Who should be encouraged to pay their overdue bills?

4. Which suppliers give the best discounts or provide the fastest services?

5. How effective was the last sales promotion?

6. How does this year (month, season) compare with the same previous period?

7. What percentage of revenue are we spending on each budget item? How can costs be reduced? Where should more money be spent?

8. What is the current ratio of assets to liabilities? Is this a safe margin? If we seem headed for trouble, what can we do about it?

Internal Controls

Our record-keeping systems have built-in controls to promote accuracy, honesty, and efficiency. These controls exist at many points in the bookkeeping cycle.

To be sure of honest accounting, we divide the responsibility so that one person's work is checked against another's. No one person has total responsibility for handling cash and also for keeping the records of cash expenditures.

We use special journals (for example, sales and expenses) for efficiency. With more than one journal, at least two people can be working on the books at once. Also, special journals increase efficiency because all data on one kind of business action is collected in one place.

Components of the Record-Keeping System

The four components of our record-keeping system are people, records, equipment, and procedures.

Source documents, papers, forms, journals, ledgers, and other records are used to keep data and to improve controls. Our documents are designed to improve efficiency. We use prenumbered forms to stimulate honesty and preprinted forms to improve accuracy. We use a combination of manual and computerized systems.

MAILMART COMPANY POLICY MANUAL

Part 5—Policies for Working Relationships

Bias in the Workplace

In almost any career, you have to work with other people. Two basic factors influence your relationships with them:

1. your background—self-identity, values, and ethnic, racial, and religious groups,

2. and the background of others.

People are different. When they work in teams—which is essential in most careers—there are tensions. Recognize it. Accept it. Bias is a fact that will be around for some time to come. The point is not to let it affect your on-the-job relationships.

Relate to Others as Individuals

When working with a person of another group, try to understand that person as an individual.

Wipe all labels, good or bad, from your mind. Say to yourself, "here is another individual, a human being. This person has the same basic needs I have and probably has similar goals." Evaluate the person on the basis of your day-to-day experiences.

You may decide the person has bad work habits or is annoying in some way. You may not want to become friends. That is all right if your decision is based on daily, fair evaluation and not on bias. By regarding the person as an individual and not a member of this or that group, the chances are you will develop a good working relationship even if you never become close friends.

Biased or Preferential Treatment

Some people make the mistake of thinking they must bend over backward to be nice to members of every group. They think they should not see anything wrong or unpleasant in anyone. People who play this game are as guilty of bias as those who think minority-group members are all bad. They still are treating people of other groups differently, rather than treating everyone the same.

Become Aware of Bias

An out-and-out display of bias is so obvious and so likely to trigger an immediate and unwanted response that most people are careful to control it. But less obvious forms of bias can also destroy good relations on the job. This is true whether bias is displayed in a negative way or through well-meaning efforts to make allowances.

Many phrases that people use unthinkingly when they talk to minorities reflect bias and can be annoying to the receiver:

I thought all you people liked . . .
How do you people feel about . . .
Gee, you did a good job for a . . .
That comes naturally for you . . .

Ethnic or racial humor—jokes whose points revolve around supposed characteristics of a particular group—can be especially offensive. Using such humor in general situations is unkind.

Women are particular victims of a continuing, unthinking bias on the part of men. Many men think that women like to be flirted with. These men think it is all right to call women pet names or address terms of endearment to them. It is not all right in the workplace.

Do Not Patronize Others

If you are a member of a minority group, you may feel especially angry when people *patronize* you, that is, treat you as a child and give you special handling. Everyone hates to be patronized; it is quite offensive.

People with foreign accents are often patronized. Some well-meaning but uninformed people will talk with them in a loud voice or use simple expressions that are almost baby talk. Just because people speak with an accent is no reason to suppose they are hard of hearing or unintelligent.

Avoiding the outright expression of bias is fairly easy. But you must also guard against patronizing attitudes that can destroy good public relations on the job.